# HEALING OF PURPOSE

# HEALING OF PURPOSE
## GOD'S CALL TO DISCIPLESHIP

# John E. Biersdorf

ABINGDON PRESS • Nashville

HEALING OF PURPOSE

*Copyright © 1985 by John E. Biersdorf*

This book is printed on acid-free paper.

**Library of Congress Cataloging in Publication Data**

Biersdorf, John, E., 1930-
  Healing of purpose.
    1. Christian life—1960-    .    2. Prayer.
3. Pastoral theology. I. Title.
BV4501.2.B47 1985        248'.5        85-9189

**ISBN 0-687-16741-8 (pbk. : alk. paper)**

MANUFACTURED BY THE PARTHENON PRESS AT
NASHVILLE, TENNESSEE, UNITED STATES OF AMERICA

*For Ruth,*
*whose enthusiasm gave me*
*courage to complete the task*

# PREFACE

This book is a gift. It is a gift from the community identified by the name of the Institute for Advanced Pastoral Studies. In that community the vision presented in this book was generated, tested, struggled for, prayed over, and celebrated. Those responsible include the seven brave souls who first entered a new unaccredited Doctor of Ministry Program in 1978 and all those who followed after them. I want again to thank Gardiner Perry, who gave me the title of one of his mini-projects to be the title of this book.

The staff of the Institute made essential contributions to it as well, arguing over and testing the ideas, and typing and re-typing the interminable drafts of the manuscript and its predecessors under different titles. Of all those who helped I especially want to express my gratitude to Joyce Holbrook, who as a volunteer did library research, took and organized careful and beautiful notes and typed the first draft of the manuscript; and Maxine Jacobs, who lovingly typed and organized subsequent drafts.

The book would not have appeared without the support and critique of colleagues in ministry. I will always be grateful to Bob Raines and Alan Green who encouraged me to complete and publish the manuscript when I had almost given up the task. Douglass Lewis, Walter Wink, Parker Palmer, and Earl Brewer also have their important place in my private pantheon of gratitude. My family was also essential. Ruth's excitement over the book enabled me to take hope for it as well. I also learned from the dialogue of life with my sons, Mark, Steve, and Dan.

It has been a difficult birth. Writing is remarkably satisfying and frustrating for me. Facing the paper pad with a pencil day by day, rewriting drafts over and over again that seemed pretty good to me until I saw them through someone else's perspective—all this would have been too much to accomplish without the prevailing sense that the ideas had a life of their own and demanded to be articulated, even if by someone as clumsy as I.

This book is a gift to seminary faculty, students, and church officials who are concerned about and have responsibility for formation for ministry. It is equally a gift to pastors and lay leaders and churches who call out the gifts to ministry of members of the Body of Christ and equip them for their tasks. It originates in my own personal experience and the experience of others with whom I have shared the mysterious and graceful process of owning and living calls to ministry. I hope that ultimately it will be helpful to many Christians wishing to discern how their faith calls them to act.

# CONTENTS

# INTRODUCTION

And Jesus came and said to them, "All authority in heaven and on earth has been given to me. Go therefore and make disciples of all nations, baptizing them in the name of the Father and of the Son and of the Holy Spirit, teaching them to observe all that I have commanded you; and lo, I am with you always, to the close of the age." *(Matthew 28:18-20)*

The purpose of this book is to explore how we respond to the imperative of Jesus Christ. We claim in faith that Christ calls us and empowers us to discipling: to be formed as disciples ourselves and to participate with Christ in the discipling of others, taking our modest and necessary place in the great cosmic drama of redemption announced in the New Testament. In discipling, the community of the church is created, and persons are called and equipped to specific roles as laity and clergy within it. Discipling is both salvation and ministry: knowing God and participating in God's mission in the world. The interest of this book is in how discipling happens.

11

How are persons called into the full life of discipleship—a process that simultaneously creates the
community of the church, brings persons into the life
of faith, and equips them as laity and clergy for
mission and ministry?

That process has had a succession of different names
and institutional embodiments through Christian
history. In the early centuries there were no specialized institutions developed for the purpose. The one
great formation process was the one all catechumens
shared, culminating in baptism at the great Easter
liturgy. Persons came to positions of specific ministries
in the very act of doing the ministry and mission of the
church as the community discerned and recognized
their gifts. Augustine, as noted later, was directly
ordained priest from his life as a layman. What
training there was for both laity and clergy, as Paul
notes, came from intimate friendship and apprenticeship with those experienced in ministry.

Later names for the enterprise, such as *priestly
formation, theological education,* and *education for
ministry* all refer to a specific approach and tradition
for equipping persons for ministry. Each term, as will
be described later, implies a theological understanding of preparation for ministry, as expressed in
characteristic institutions and human interactions.
In this book I want to suggest that discipling is a
*healing of purpose.* I believe that healing of purpose is
an important contemporary way to understand how
God in Christ calls and empowers us into the fullness
of faith and, in doing so, equips community and
persons for mission and ministry.

The plan of this book originates from this conviction. The first chapter suggests the term *healing of
purpose* as a way of understanding Jesus' own calling
of the disciples and equipping them for ministry.

Jesus' own ministry in this respect is the foundation and most important criterion for discipling. The church's subsequent institutions and programs for this purpose explicitly or implicitly measure themselves against this standard. They are, to be precise, metaphors of Jesus' calling of the disciples. Chapters 2, 3, and 4 explore three historic metaphors for discipling. A metaphor in this sense is a human endeavor meant to be a faithful and revelatory likeness of the mystery of God's direct intervention in human lives and history through Jesus Christ. Chapters 5, 6, and 7 look at the cultural changes that make a new metaphor for discipling needed and important. Chapter 8 names and outlines that new metaphor. The last four chapters describe how that new metaphor is a healing of purpose, calling us to the fullness of mission and ministry.

I hope the book will be useful to all, clergy and laity, who seek a vitality and fullness of Christian life and ministry. I want to write for those who seek and demand a fresh sense of the presence of God and who believe that prayer and ministry are not opposites, but the single experience of that presence.

# HEALING OF PURPOSE

# CHAPTER ONE

# Healing of Purpose

Passing along by the Sea of Galilee, he saw Simon and
Andrew the brother of Simon casting a net in the sea, for
they were fishermen. And Jesus said to them, "Follow me
and I will make you become fishers of men." (*Mark 1:16-17;
cf. Matthew 4:18-20*)

The account in both Matthew and Mark follows the
same sequence: Jesus' baptism by John, the
temptations in the wilderness, and his first proclama-
tion of the gospel. He then calls James and John, the
sons of Zebedee, also to follow him, whereupon he
immediately enters the synagogue at Capernaum on
the sabbath (in Mark) and begins to proclaim the
gospel and to heal. Is there a way to get beyond the
pun and the simple Sunday school lesson to see the
mystery of God as a human being encountering and
transforming singular human beings? Probably on
the written page the best we can do is to suggest that
God walked on the beach that day. *God* walked on the
beach and met four men and something of incredible
mystery happened between them. If we are to have

any hope of even partially apprehending that event, we must approach it as mystery. I cannot imagine what it would be like for God to walk up to me on the street as I am entering Chatham's in Birmingham and change my life, just like that.

I want to resist the temptation to label the story with a theological or educational abstraction and concentrate on the mystery a bit longer. It is like coming to an insight in counseling. I know it is an important insight because my body relaxes and shifts in my depths, and I can watch the insight itself disappear in the forgetfulness of repression. It seems easier to just forget, and much more difficult to focus, to contemplate, to pay attention just a bit longer to the mystery of God's grace working in my life. So it is when we encounter scripture, or more precisely, when scripture encounters us. What is it we must continue to focus on to see God walking in our lives?

What is there is this outrageous pun: "Follow me and I will make you become fishers of men." It isn't even funny. It seems strained. What connection is Jesus making between killing fish for economic survival and becoming a disciple, or being called to ministry? Probably studying the literal meaning of the words—abstracted from the human-divine encounter—will not get us much deeper into the mystery. Somehow Jesus met these men and drew for them a connection between who they were and what they did in the context of fishing for a living and who they essentially or potentially could be and do in the context of following Christ. How can we understand that?

Alfred North Whitehead was the first philosopher who understood the world of modern physics and the mathematics that makes it possible. For him, God in God's antecedent nature is all the potential in the universe. Every possibility that could ever be in time or eternity already is present in God. Each entity in the universe actualizes some of that potential every time it makes a decision. Simon and Andrew and James and John actualize some of the potential life available to them as they decide to be fishermen and to fish that day. And other possibilities are overlooked by them or are not available in the context of fishing or are denied in the inevitable pain and suffering of their lives.

God in God's consequent nature for Whitehead is the love that draws us to the fulfillment of our potential. Jesus walked on the beach that day and *saw* Simon and Andrew and James and John—saw them not as their wives or customers saw them, nor even as they saw themselves. He saw them as God saw them; saw their full potential, partially realized and partially denied in their life decisions. He saw what may be called their *purpose*, the essential unique possibility for which they were created and which could only be actualized in their life decisions.

Seeing that purpose, he called to it. He called in a way that may be termed *healing* their purpose. He gave a context, a presence in which their deciding could heal their past denials of their potential and could complete its future fulfillment. They could not see and therefore could not heal their purpose by themselves. Their limitations, their pain, their confusion prevented that. Jesus, in calling to their purpose, healed it by disclosing it to them and providing a context or presence in which they could decide to realize it. Jesus, in his healing call, affirmed who they had been as fishermen and who they could be as disciples.

To call this divine-human encounter the "healing of purpose" does not mean in any way to have explained the mystery. It only means to have penetrated as far as possible into it to some partial discernment. *Healing of purpose* seems a useful term to indicate what Jesus was about in calling the disciples and, therefore, what ministerial formation can be.

The encounter with the fishermen disciples is preceded by the healing of Jesus' own purpose in both Matthew and Mark. The account opens with the intriguing words, "Then Jesus was led by the Spirit out into the wilderness to be tempted by the devil" (Matthew 4:1 JB). The gospel writers thus imply the Spirit conspired with Satan to test Jesus. Who is this Satan who evidently is in cahoots with God's Spirit? John Sanford, in a careful study of the Hebrew and Greek words used in the scripture, concludes that Satan means the adversary, i.e., one who blocks forward movement. What or who is it that blocks forward movement for the newly baptized Lord? The blocks seem to be temptations to alternative, limited, and guaranteed understandings of his purpose. Each is tested in the encounter between God's Spirit and the person of Jesus. The result is a healing of purpose. Jesus decides that his own ministry is neither a repetition of guaranteed and stereotyped roles from prophecy nor a satisfaction of his human needs, but a moment-by-moment discernment and dependence on the guidance of the Spirit.

"You must worship the Lord your God, and serve him alone" (Matthew 4:10*b* JB). Satan, as Walter Wink has said, is yesterday's will of God. It is tempting for us to project Satan as an external center of will who blocks our deciding to live for God. In truth the enemy is ourselves, i.e., our own will expressed in decisions to live for skewed, limited, and secure purposes. The healing of purpose, for Jesus and for us, is to decide to live in God's present and presence.

## NAMING

We have suggested that *healing of purpose* is a useful term to indicate the mystery of Jesus' call to his disciples. Sometimes Jesus gives a name; at other times he challenges to decide or act. Both seem essential to the healing of purpose. First, the naming, although both dimensions are intertwined in the gospel accounts. There is a different account of the calling of Andrew and Simon in the Gospel of John. There Andrew is originally a disciple of John the Baptist. After John points Jesus out as the Lamb of God, Andrew follows Jesus and brings his brother Simon to him. When he met Simon, "Jesus looked hard at him and said, 'You are Simon son of John; you are to be called Cephas'—meaning Rock" (John 1:42 JB).

The Jerusalem Bible does fairly well at translating the Greek word for Jesus' attitude toward Peter. *Emblepsas* has the character of a fixed gaze or spiritual discernment. Again our own contemplation is the best way to touch the mystery of those eyes and that look. What would it be like to have God look into our eyes? Perhaps the terror of realizing our absolute nakedness, then the deeper terror of seeing God see depths and dark places and glorious possibilities in us totally beyond our awareness. Then the incredible peace of loving acceptance transforms terror into the relief of being totally known and the joy and promise of what we can be.

Jesus looks hard at Simon, discerns his purpose and his potential, and renames him Rocky. Jesus' sense of humor sometimes seems excessive. The gospel accounts of Peter suggests a volatile, impetuous man whose strength and evident leadership are seldom disciplined. On the mount of transfiguration he runs around like an overwrought sports fan babbling about building a hall of fame for Jesus, Moses, and Elijah. Before the crucifixion he shows an ominous cowardice, and his tears of remorse seem insufficient to redeem his betrayal. El Greco paints him along with Mary Magdalene as one of the two great New Testamnt exemplars of the Counter-Reformation virtue of penance. With great, glistening eyes, he is shown crying to heaven for his sins and for another chance to be faithful.

But Jesus is not having fun at Peter's expense. God sees into Simon's heart, and by naming his essential purpose, heals it. The healing of purpose seems to involve a naming, a raising to consciousness of fundamental images of who we are and what we are to do to fulfill the potential of God's purpose for our lives. Jesus' naming of Peter is an artful disclosure to him of whom he is called to be, of who he essentially is, even though he does not know it. Now he can no longer *not* know it. The symbol of Rock is before his consciousness and beneath his consciousness. And it will not let him go until he has become whom God has meant him to be, until he is the foundation on which the church can be built and to whom the keys of heaven may be entrusted. The healing is in the promise and the challenge of the name. The name is not necessarily a visual symbol or a word. It is the clarity of purpose God elicits in us, however that may come to us. It may be the wordless sense of God's immediate guidance, as Jesus perhaps experienced at the end of the tests in the wilderness. And it will probably evolve from time to time as God discloses to us new aspects of our potential and our purpose.

## DECIDING

Jesus names. Jesus also calls us to act to realize the promise of the name. Both are essential to the healing of purpose and to education for ministry. The challenge to act occurs throughout the New Testament. One of the most poignant examples is in relation to the man who is called young in Matthew, a ruler in Luke, and wealthy in both and in Mark as well. He comes to Jesus and asks for the healing of purpose according to the custom of his religion and culture. "Good Master, what must I do to inherit eternal life?" (Mark 10:17a JB). Jesus is a tough counselor. He rebukes the man's plea to be rescued by dependency on a wise, loving authority figure. "Why do you call me good? No one is good but God alone." Then he literally reads the law to him by reciting the Decalogue. The man protests, I imagine with some annoyance, that he has kept the law in strict obedience since he was a child. And there seems no reason to doubt his claim.

Then the remarkable event happens. "And Jesus looking upon him loved him." What is the quality, the character of this divine love embodied in Jesus' eyes? We imagine that Jesus saw the surface and the depths of the man with total clarity. He saw the essential purpose for which God created him in potentiality. He saw the partial fulfillment and partial denial of that potential as he had lived it thus far. Seeing him completely he could not help but love him, for he saw the image of God in him that could not be entirely erased or obscured by his foolish actions. And therefore he recognized a brother, and he loved him.

But even further, he recognized what the healing of the man's purpose would entail. With the artfulness of God's love incarnate, he specified the action or decision that would expose his evasions and enable him to be whom he was meant to be. "You lack one thing: go, sell what you have, and give to the poor, and you will have treasure in heaven; and come, follow me" (Mark 10:21).

The action demanded is both a doing and a being. It is a doing—an instruction to use his wealth in ministry. It is equally a being—a bringing to light of the essential purpose of his life. The decision fulfills the naming, although the name is implicit here, by testing it in action.

As it turns out, the man says no instead of yes to God and himself. And he goes away sorrowful, as well he might, at betraying God and himself and missing such a significant opportunity for life. God is powerless here to coerce decision, and unwilling to manipulate it. Some will argue that Jesus was simply unskillful. Graduate training in pastoral counseling would have enabled our Lord to reflect the man's feelings more sensitively and lead him to the growth decision more effectively. But the whole point of the story would be missed that way. No and yes must both be possibilities for decision, or else we will never own our purpose as ours. The healing of purpose requires both our decision and God's grace, and the intimate collaboration of the two.

We have called naming and deciding two aspects of the healing of purpose as seen in our Lord's actions in calling his disciples and sending them forth in mission. We have said that our Lord's actions provide our fundamental understanding of discipling, which is both a call to faith and an equipping for ministry. There is nothing we can recognize as preparation in these stories. There is no schooling, no interim between receiving the call or name and testing it in action. In fact, as in the case of the Gerasene demoniac, when the healed one pleads for a time to be with Jesus to assimilate and rejoice in his wholeness, our Lord explicitly tells him to get on with action—telling the good news to the Gentiles in the Decapolis. That does not mean that Jesus abandoned him or us. His promise is to be with us, but not necessarily in seminary.

### After the Crucifixion

We have so far focused on God's embodied actions in Jesus for clues to understanding ministerial formation. There is great discontinuity between his earthly career and the later life of the church. Whether one reads the panic in the original ending of Mark or the serene promises at the end of the other gospels, it is clear that the disciples simply did not know what to do or how to live when Jesus was no longer with them in bodily form. He had promised, according to the traditions, that Another would come and teach all things and bring to remembrance all that Jesus had said (John 14:26). But what those promises meant must have been a mystery.

According to the first chapter of Acts, the disciples remained together in hope and anticipation of the fulfillment of the promises Jesus made before the crucifixion and after the resurrection when he was spiritually present with them in some way. The fulfillment came in a miracle of communication. Reversing the symbolism of the tower of Babel, Pentecost revealed the Holy Spirit enabling human beings again to communicate with each other across the boundaries of language, nation, and race. Peter preached the church's first sermon, and three thousand souls heard it, understood it, and were baptized in Christ.

Here was a continuation of Jesus' ministry on a massive communal scale. The apostles, filled with the Holy Spirit, are able to continue Jesus' work through preaching and healing. The healing of purpose continues to come to both individuals and groups. The difference now is that the locus of the healing is the community of those baptized in Christ, called the church, instead of the singular God-man Jesus. When the three thousand are baptized, "they devoted themselves to the apostles' teaching and fellowship, to the breaking of bread and the prayers" (Acts 2:42). This reference to the church is further amplified:

And all who believed were together and had all things in common; and they sold their possessions and goods and distributed them to all, as any had need. And day by day, attending the temple together and breaking bread in their homes, they partook of food with glad and generous hearts, praising God and having favor with all the people. And the Lord added to their number day by day those who were being saved. (Acts 2:44-47)

The naming comes through the preaching and healing; the deciding comes through the corporate actions of the Christian community to hold all things in common and to give to those in need. Jesus Christ through the Holy Spirit continues to abide with them in the Christian community for the healing of purpose. The breaking of bread (the early eucharist) and the prayers continue the earthly conversations of Jesus. Christ now guides the church and its members through the spiritual conversation of prayer and communion as he once did walking beside them in bodily form. The Spirit calls out specific persons, confers names or gifts, and calls them to test their gifts in decision and action in the corporate ministry of the church.

> To each is given the manifestation of the Spirit for the common good. To one is given through the Spirit the utterance of wisdom, and to another the utterance of knowledge by the same Spirit, to another faith by the same Spirit, to another gifts of healing by the one Spirit, to another the working of miracles, to another prophecy, to another the ability to distinguish between spirits, to another various kinds of tongues, to another the interpretation of tongues. All these are inspired by one and the same Spirit, who apportions to each one individually as he wills. (I Corinthians 12:7-11)

We probably best understand this passage not as a catalogue of general offices in the church, but as the continuation of Christ's ministry of calling to the essential purpose and potential of singular human beings, naming their purpose and challenging them to act it out in mission. The essential difference is that the naming and the deciding are now in the community of the church.

At least this is our faith—that Christ is with us as surely and immediately present in the church as he was with the disciples in Galilee. Actually, he is with us even more, because through the crucifixion and resurrection we now understand his revelation in its completeness in a way the disciples could not before those events. We believe that Christ through the Holy Spirit speaks to us through the preaching, sacraments, prayers, and common life of the church as immediately as he spoke on the beach that day to Andrew and Simon and the sons of Zebedee. At least that is our belief.

In practice we are not so sure. As it turns out, sometimes it seems to happen, and sometimes it doesn't, from the age of the apostles to our own. Sometimes the Spirit is so palpably present among us that the preaching and the healing are as obviously effective as Peter's on the day of Pentecost. Sometimes the light is so dim that only certain beliefs in the correctness of what we are doing or a willingness to suffer the evident absence of God keeps us going. Whatever our experience, our intention is to faithfully continue our Lord's healing of purpose in the church. We intend that our formation be a likeness of Jesus' calling and empowering of the disciples. How the church has gone about creating that likeness is the topic of the next chapter.

# CHAPTER TWO

# Augustine: Can We Love God?

Through the history of the church there has been a series of implicit or explicit attempts to create a likeness between Jesus' calling and empowering of the disciples and certain activities of the church for the same purpose. These likenesses are metaphors, present activities which we hope remind us of, illumine, and re-present Jesus' acts of discipling. There are a number of metaphors in the history of the church for the healing of purpose. Three of them are especially important resources and blocks for God's call to mission and ministry in contemporary life.

In order to explore them, we need to understand how metaphors, especially religious metaphors, function. Sallie McFague suggests that metaphors unite and subsume: subjective and objective, concrete and

abstract, and other analytic categories in the more
important contrast between familiar and strange.

> The familiar (Bultmann's 'pre-understanding;' if you
> will)—common experiences and everyday words—is the
> means for grasping the unfamiliar, but the connections
> between these two dimensions are rung in such a way
> (the way poets ring them) that the strange and
> unfamiliar (Barth's action of God on behalf of his people,
> if you will) breaks apart and renovates the familiar. The
> significant categories are not subjective and objective,
> but old and new (old wineskins and new wine, the old
> man Adam and the new man Jesus, old creation and new
> creation, death and life)—accepted patterns and new
> interpretations, clichés and new meaning, old facts and
> new insight into them. (Sallie McFague, *Speaking in
> Parables* [Philadelphia: Fortress Press, 1975], p. 32)

The metaphor works both ways: it illumines "the
principal subject," or strange partner of the metaphor,
e.g., God, by seeing it through the grid or lens of the
familiar "subsidiary subject," e.g., father. But perhaps
even more important, religious metaphors especially
illumine and transform a facet of ordinary life by
juxtaposition with the transcendent. McFague claims
that in metaphorical constructions in scripture, "what
we learn is not primarily something about God but a
new way to live ordinary life" (p. 45). The metaphor is an
embodied, lived reality, which must be encountered in
all its detail; in which the moment of insight and the
choice of metaphor are all part of an artful possibility of
emotional impact and cognitive meaning.

Discussion of metaphor in contemporary Christian
theology focuses upon metaphor in language. But
metaphor is more than a linguistic device. It is,
according to Elizabeth Sewell, "the human method
of investigating the universe" (ibid., p. 59). Ian
Barbour suggests that scientific models are best

understood as the rigorous and detailed use of a metaphor. An example encompasses the theories regarding the nature of light. Light was first scientifically understood by analogy with ocean waves. It behaved in a fashion best described by the metaphor, "Light is a wave (of water, as in an ocean)." Further data did not fit the comparison, and a new metaphor was developed: "Light is composed of particles (like billiard balls)." Finally physicists concluded that both metaphors need to be used in complementary fashion to understand the nature of light: "Light is wave-like *and* particle-like." Complementary metaphors are often necessary to guide the understanding of complex physical phenomena. Metaphors in science also function to make complex mathematical formulae understandable and to suggest further development of the formulae to explain the phenomena to which they refer.

Metaphors in religious use need to remain close to the ground. They are not expendable, except for communication purposes, when the theory is fully developed, as in science. There is no way around the metaphor, for it itself is a sacramental, embodied way by which we can touch divine reality—or, more significantly, by which grace can touch us. McFague writes, "We do not interpret the parable, the parable interprets us" (p. 71). The parable as a metaphor is an invitation for our own lives to be interpreted or illumined in the light of transcendent reality. The religious metaphor is not a means of passive understanding or prediction and control of external reality; it is a call to decision. The metaphors of the Christian faith do not attempt to *explain* divine reality; they attempt to enable us to *participate* in it and disclose God in a fresh way. Jesus' phrase "our Father in heaven" does not explain God. Explanation

implies prediction, control, and analytical knowledge. Jesus, and we, intend none of these when we use
the phrase. We use it not to try to analyze or control
God, but to *pray* to God. Pray means to communicate
with and participate in the presence of God.
Metaphors in religious use are symbols, i.e., they
participate in a reality beyond themselves to which
they point. When we pray "our Father in heaven," we
hope through the words to touch God, to be in God's
presence.

### METAPHOR AND TIME

In our culture, we have certain peculiar ideas about
time which probably make this use of metaphors
impossible to take seriously as long as we remain
with them. We believe, because of the heritage of
Western science, that linear time is an absolute
context within which we live. Time passes, according
to the clocks we have developed, as a totally accurate
picture of reality. No event can be repeated, and once
gone, it is lost forever. Our lives and our anxieties are
ruled by our unthinking faith in the ticks or digital
readouts beside our beds, on our wrists, and around
us in every public place.

Within this view of the world, what the church does
about discipling is in the present and Jesus' calling of
the disciples is in the past of two millennia. The only
connection between them is the dubious idea that
somehow Jesus stayed around in some ghostly
fashion after the resurrection and now calls John
Jones into ministry in some way similar to his calling
Peter on the beach two thousand years ago. But they
are two discrete events. Then he was a human being;
now he is a ghost. The metaphor no longer is a
participation in Christ but a memory of him. The

metaphor loses its essential meaning and force. The tendency is to pay close attention to the human activities we have designed for equipping the saints for ministry and relegate the memory of Christ to the rhetoric at the morning chapel or the ordination service in case we have forgotten something.

Primitive human beings, according to Mircea Eliade in *The Myth of the Eternal Return*, had a very different understanding of time in their sacred rituals.

> A sacrifice, for example, not only exactly reproduces the initial sacrifice revealed by a god *ab origine*, at the beginning of time, it also takes place at the same primordial mythical moment; in other words, every sacrifice repeats the original sacrifice and coincides with it. All sacrifices are performed at the same mythical instant of the beginning; through the paradox of rite, profane time and duration are suspended. (Larry Dossey, *Space, Time and Medicine* [Boulder and London: Shambhala Press, 1982], pp. 28 ff).

Since we are modern human beings, we may not be impressed by what primitive people thought. But the world view of modern physics is startlingly like it in some respects. Linear time is no longer the absolute context for the world. It is rather an artifact we have constructed under certain cultural influences to make sense out of our experience. For the physicist, "the flow of time is clearly an inappropriate concept for the description of the physical world that has no past, present and future. It just is" (ibid., p. 31). Our conscious thoughts of how events are arranged in time come from our processing of sense impressions, not from external events themselves.

That concept, which is at the heart of the special theory of relativity, is apt by itself to give us vertigo.

But when we reflect upon it, it coincides with our common human experience. When we are with our beloved or deeply engrossed in a creative task, our time sense can dramatically change. Hours of clock time can pass, and we have experienced only moments of intense joy and satisfaction. When we are bored the opposite is true, and the minute hand seems to be simply stuck.

Two thousand years of linear time is not an absolute chasm separating our present discipling activities from the activities of Jesus. We are not condemned to dismiss metaphor because of our modern belief in the illusion of the absoluteness of linear time. Nor do we need to adopt the primitive belief in the exact repetition of timeless events. We can instead understand the church's programs aimed at growth in laity and ministry as metaphors in which both the uniqueness of these activities and their participation in the actual ministry of Christ are affirmed.

### CHARACTERISTICS OF METAPHOR

The present partner of the metaphor, the formation and education programs we construct, includes environments or settings, processes, and content. One can think of the settings of the desert Eremites, the monastic communities, the Counter-Reformation seminary, the German university. Each setting has its own structure of physical space, provision of material needs, and interaction and isolation from the larger environment. Each environment for ministry formation characteristically expresses the values of the metaphor and molds the experiences of its participants.

Human processes are the second necessary way to

understand a metaphor for education for ministry. From clinical pastoral education group therapy sessions to chanting the psalms in choir, names are given and decisions are made in characteristic interactions. Finally content, from visual images to abstract written formulations, makes conscious and explicit the often more powerful implicit metaphorical statements of environment and process. Together, the three aspects of a metaphor communicate its intended participation in the ministry of Christ.

Metaphors are erected in the intersection of contemporary cultural beliefs and ways of thinking, available institutional forms, and the paradigmatic struggles of particular persons and communities to be healed of purpose and live in Christ. It is fair to say they appear. The mysterious interaction with God's grace, to paraphrase Heidegger, provides a clearing, an open space in human experience. The healing of purpose appears in a fresh way, and its shining draws people and energy to its further development. It grows to the maturity of clear theory and specific institutions formed to express the metaphor. It dies or is radically altered as it loses touch with cultural issues and divine-human experience.

In Christian history, a small number of metaphors have guided the church's attempts to fulfill the great commission of Christ. Though expressed in many different institutional forms, there are only a few basic ways to approach the question of how God calls us to mission and ministry. There seems to be three basic metaphors, lived out in many variations, underlying the church's institutions and programs.

Each fundamental metaphor can be named with a basic question, some historical version of the rich young ruler's question to Jesus. Because each metaphor intends to involve Christ's answer in a

certain cultural and institutional context, it responds
to the typical human way of asking, in that context,
the fundamental question, "What must I do to inherit
eternal life?"

The first metaphor is exemplified in the passions
and life of Augustine, and was distinctly shaped by
him. I want to characterize his question to the Lord in
this way, "Can we love God?" In the Catholic
tradition, the heart has been the symbol of Saint
Augustine (Eugene Portalie, S. J., *A Guide to the
Thought of St. Augustine* [Chicago: Henry Regnery,
1960], p. 305). In the painfully honest struggles of this
magnificent man and in his profound theoretical
formulations, the question is displayed, "How can
the disorderly will and affections be brought to love
the immutable eternal God?"

He outlines much of the theology underlying
the metaphor in the opening paragraph of his
*Confessions*:

> [M]an, that bears about him his mortality, the witness of
> his sin, . . . yet would man praise Thee; he, but a particle
> of Thy creation. Thou awakest us to delight in Thy
> praise; for Thou madest us for Thyself, and our heart is
> restless, until it repose in Thee. . . . but how shall they
> call on Him in whom they have not believed? or how
> shall they believe without a preacher? . . . I will seek
> Thee, Lord, by calling on Thee; and will call on Thee,
> believing in Thee; for to us hast thou been preached. My
> faith, Lord, shall call on Thee, which Thou hast given
> me, wherewith Thou hast inspired me, through the
> Incarnation of Thy Son, through the ministry of the
> Preacher. (*The Confessions of St. Augustine*, trans.
> Edward B. Pusey [New York: Random House, The
> Modern Library, 1949], pp. 3,4)

The God he wishes to know and to love is both the
God of Plato and Aristotle, and the God of the

Hebrews and of Jesus Christ. He finds his own salvation in the complex and even profoundly forced integration of the two traditions.

The God he wishes to know is the eternal One of which the universe, according to Plato, is the moving image (*eikon*). In spite of his hatred for Greek as a boy (*Confessions*, p. 15), Augustine absorbed the Greek understanding of God from the culture of his time and explicitly adopted it from the Neoplatonists while teaching at Milan (Portalie, *Guide*, p. 12). As he articulates it in the *Confessions* (12.11), "You have already told me, Lord, loudly in my inner ear, that you are eternal and also have immortality, since you never change in form or through motion; nor is your will modified in time" (Robert E. Meagher, *An Introduction to Augustine* [New York: New York University Press, 1978], p. 212). Perfect, unchangeable, eternal Being itself reposes without motion in essential unity beneath all forms, changes, and the multiplicity of the phenomenal world.

This grand beatific vision of essential unity underlying all the multiplicity of human experience guided mystical experience and philosophical thought not just for Augustine, and not even only for the world of his time. It is one enduring possibility across religions and cultures and world history for the deepest experience of reality of which human beings are capable. For those who have in some way even dimly apprehended that unity, the usual perceptions and activities of life seem trivial, distracting, and to be put aside as far as possible. Eternal, unchangeable unity is as intriguing for philosophical thought as it is for religious experience. Our logic seeks coherence amidst disorder and unity beneath variety. To conclude that the universe itself supports our human desire for simplicity and order, or even further, that ultimate reality *is* that unity, is to know a salvation available to philosophers.

How can one know such a God? In Greek thought, "the activity of the senses provides the paradigm and the actual foundation for the activity of the mind" (ibid., p. 14). Of the senses, sight, above all, discloses what the mind is and how it operates. Perhaps one would have to live in a setting as dominated by the sun as Greece is, amidst a culture steeped since before human memory in that fierce and benevolent light, to understand such a statement. The experience of seeing is formative for Greek thought and shapes its understanding of the human condition in a very different way than if touch or hearing had evolved as a primary paradigm. Seeing is passive in a way that touch is not. We can observe without motion or activity on our part. We simply receive without doing violence or even participating in that which we observe. The passivity of seeing, however, is also its power to control. In hearing we must wait patiently or impatiently for the temporal passing of a narrow auditory channel of information. In seeing we can grasp the whole at once, scan great amounts of information, and understand it, i. e., order it into a coherent pattern. The eye of the mind is thus able to control the disorderly multiplicity of life by ordering it, by seeing the essence or patterns or underlying unity. Finally, it is spatial, not temporal like hearing or touch, and therefore timeless. We can see the persistence of form or idea through movement and variation and therefore conceive of the eternal.

The mind is like seeing. The eye does not see itself, but the images in its environment. In the same way, the mind is not an entity to be known by itself. According to Aristotle, "The mind *is nothing* before it 'minds' (*noein*) and then it is one, one activity, one unfolding life (*mia energeia*) with what it 'minds' or knows." The proper function of the mind is "the receiving and the imaging of all things, not in their multiplicity, but in their unity" (ibid., pp. 17-18). The mind is to passively receive from its environment and passively control that reception by seeing, i.e., understanding, the unity underlying the plethora of perceptions. What is essential is the perception of images *as* images. Thus the mind discloses the truth of the whole. "Disclosure is a dialectic, an unfolding vision which leads the see-er, insight by insight, from unreality to reality, from image to original, from nonbeing to being, from the many to the one" (ibid., p. 16). Thus the mind knows God through the passive seeing of the perfection of God's unity through the multiplicity of the phenomenal world.

And this is the proper purpose, nature, and end of the mind and of human beings—to see God. For Aristotle and for Augustine, the nature of a thing is its end, i.e., what each thing is when its becoming is complete. Speech has its part to play here as well. For speech is the distinctively human activity of marking out the boundaries or limits between what is real and what is not, between being and nonbeing. In seeing God, we also see or discover our own true nature, which is to see God. Like the mind or the eye, our true reality is not to behold ourselves, but to behold God; and thus realize our own reality, which is to be a beholder of God. Our proper human activity is to become this purpose or end. It is "largely a passivity in which a human being is led to its own disclosure as it speechfully discloses the reality of the universe, or the whole." Speech, however, being temporal, must also pass away in the final ecstasy of the pure beholding of the eternal. The soul does not speak and

God does not speak in wordless contemplation, according to the Greeks (ibid., pp. 16, 19).

This is true blessedness, *beatitudo*, one of Augustine's favorite words, and the proper end or purpose of human nature: to see the eternal, unchanging God. It is the highest human work and the consummation of Augustine's own passionate human struggle. The problem is that it is not so easy to do. For we human beings are temporal, not eternal, and we invariably get lost in the multiplicity of the creation and do not see the unity of the Creator. Instead of going within to behold the One, we become distracted with externals. The essential problem here seems to be one of will. It may be possible to passively behold the One, although even reason falters at this point and is not consistent. But our will or desires or loves get in the way. For we follow what we love, which seldom is the wordless contemplation of God. Augustine writes, "Humankind goes outside itself to follow what it creates, abandoning him within by whom it was created and destroying what it was made to be" (*Confessions* 10.35, quoted in Meagher, *Introduction*, p. 163).

The verbs shift in this conversation, from knowing to loving, and from seeing to doing. Our loves distract us from knowing, our activity or doing prevents our passivity or seeing. What we love, we do, and our actions come to determine our character, who we are. "One's love determines one's person, and one's person determines one's love. What I love is both constitutive and expressive of who I am, of what kind of person I am" (ibid., p. 100). This circularity of character and conduct further enmeshes us in the things of the world and takes us further from God. Finally we become trapped in the idolatries we have created. "By refusing to serve, they do not avoid serving altogether but avoid only the service of the Lord. For if anyone will not serve love, that person will, of necessity, serve evil" (*Expositions on the Psalms* 18.2.15, quoted in Meagher, *Introduction*, p. 109). Our loves determine who we are and enslave us in our pursuit of them.

Our love of the things of this world, and our inability to see and love God through them, is not absolute evil, but the turning away from the greater good for the lesser; "sin or iniquity is not the desiring of evil natures but the abandoning of better things" (*On the Nature of the Good* 34, quoted in Meagher, *Introduction*, p. 165). How do we turn from the lesser to the greater? We cannot do it unaided. We need a gracious God, Hebrew rather than Greek this time, who can stoop to our condition, coming from the eternal to the temporal to lead us in faith back to the eternal:

> Since we were incapable of seizing eternal things, and since we were weighed down by the vileness of our sins, contracted by our love of temporal things and growing in us as if naturally from the shoot of our morality, we need to be cleansed. But it was only through temporal things that we could be cleansed so as to be ruled with eternal things. . . .
>
> Truth itself, coeternal with the father, has had its beginning from the earth (Psalm 84:12) when the son of God came as that he might become the son of man and that he might take to himself our faith, thereby to lead us to his truth. He assumed our mortality in such a way as not to lose his own eternity. (*On the Trinity* 4.18.24, quoted in Meagher, *Introduction*, pp. 219-20)

The God of Jesus Christ is not solitary and indifferent as is the Greek God, but compassionate and able to come to us in our temporality and estrangement of will. The great gift he brings to us is the gift of faith, which enables us to believe in God even when we do not know him. By faith we are enabled to love him, and thus to know him.

> We have not seen him but we are to see him; we have not known him but we are to know him. We believe in him whom we have not known. Or is it perhaps that we have known from faith but have not yet known from sight . . . Now, while on pilgrimage, we walk by faith and not by sight (II Corinthians 5:7). Thus our righteousness too is through faith and not through sight. Our righteousness will be perfect when we shall see by actual beholding." (*Tracts on the First Epistle of John* 4.8, quoted in Meagher, *Introduction*, p. 255)

The way to God is by faith in Jesus Christ, who purifies us from our loves of the world and leads us back to the proper love of God, and therefore knowing of God. Jesus is both example and assurance that such ascent to God is possible. In eternity and truth he comes to our temporal condition and by faith leads us back to the realm of truth. "Our faith is as far removed from the clear sight of truth as is our mortality removed from eternity." Because of Jesus Christ, however, "truth prevails over faith as eternity prevails over what has a beginning" (*On the Trinity* 4.18.24, quoted in Meagher, *Introduction*, p. 220). The Word made flesh in Jesus and in scripture is definitive speech. Not like pagan speech which is limited and must fall silent before the truth of contemplation, the speech of scripture is truth itself. Thus in the revelation of Christ, knowledge and faith are finally joined in a word at once eternal and temporal.

Having heard the word we find our way back to God through acts of faith, believing in the content of faith in Christ. Augustine's trinity of human capabilities—memory, understanding, and will—becomes the means of doing so. Holding Christ in memory, contemplating Christ with our understanding, loving Christ with our will, we seek the eternal God in this temporal life. We intend to love temporal things, including ourselves and others, only for the sake of God. "None of us are to enjoy ourselves, if you perceive clearly, because we ought not to love ourselves for our own sakes, but rather for the sake of him who is to be enjoyed. . . . Then no other human beings should be incensed if you love them for the sake of God" (*On Christian Instruction* 1.22.20-23, quoted in Meagher, *Introduction*, p. 187). But our faith is partial, a continuing struggle. Augustine confesses as a mature man, "And still my soul is sad, because it falls back and becomes an abyss, or rather because it realizes that it is still an abyss. My faith, which you have kindled in the night before my steps, my faith speaks into that abyss" (*Confessions* 13.14, quoted in Meagher, *Introduction*, p. 258).

Augustine does foresee the end of time as proclaimed in scripture, when faith shall be sight and things come to their perfection. In that final time beyond the end of time, all things—earth and sea, heavens, and the soul itself—shall fall silent,

> and if he alone should speak, not through them but through himself, so that we would hear his word . . . and if this one vision should so seize and consume and steal away the see-er in inward joys so that his life might be forever like that moment of understanding for which we sighed, would this not be: Enter into the joy of the Lord?" (Matthew 25:21 [*Confessions* 9.10, quoted in Meagher, *Introduction*, p. 288])

What would human beings *do* in that day? Works of mercy and works of necessity would no longer be appropriate since misery and necessity have passed away. Would the Christian then remain in wordless, actionless contemplation? No, says Augustine, because activity and love must not cool. God will continue to inflame our love and our ceaseless activity shall be this: the praise of God. "You will not, however, cease to love, because the one whom you see is such that he never surprises you with weariness. He both satisfies you and does not. What I am saying is wonderful" (*Expositions on the Psalms* 85.24, quoted in Meagher, *Introduction*, pp. 280-81).

The magnificent Christian vision of Augustine integrates the Eternal One and the Yahweh of compassion, bestowing knowledge and love of God through faith in Jesus Christ. The revelation of God in Christ is as perfectly suited to the human condition as the Eternal God is perfect in itself. There is one problem: the wayward, changeable, distractable human will which so easily is lost in its loves for the things of this world. In Augustine's vision, "the finite, free soul is thus the one disorderly exception in an order otherwise perfectly established" (ibid., p. 259). That disorderly exception must be the focus for exploring the metaphor for the healing purpose that evolves from Augustine's life and thought. It is disclosed in his own life, or more precisely, the story he tells of his life in the *Confessions*, written when he was in his early forties. It may seem unfair to expect a person's life to exemplify his thought, but Augustine meant it that way. In the *Confessions*, his life is a series of object lessons in the struggle of the soul to free itself from the love of external things and find its way to the proper love of God. To put it in its simplest form, the healing of purpose is a series of strategies for quieting the love of external things, thus turning the soul to its proper love of God. Augustine uses the analogy of weight. Everything is urged by its own weight to see its own place, which is its proper order. "When out of their order, they are restless; restored to order, they are at rest." One's weight is one's love. When inflamed by God's gift of faith, one's love finds its proper place and order in delighting in God. "We ascend Thy ways that be in our heart, and sing a song of degrees; we glow inwardly with Thy fire, with Thy good fire, and we go; because we go upwards to the peace of Jerusalem" (*Confessions*, p. 307).

How does one quiet one's restless will, that it may find its proper weight or love of God? The twofold prescription is quite straightforward: "We must take flight entirely from things of sense" and "the general love of action, which turns the soul away from what is true, proceeds from pride" (Meagher, *Introduction*, pp. 190, 165). Sensual enjoyment and the love of action are the two manifestations of the restless will which must be curbed.

Proceeding from these premises, then, Augustine remorsefully demonstrates their power in his life and his heroic, prayerful, and often unsuccessful attempts to curb them that he might be turned to the love and praise of God. His extravagant remorse over stealing pears in an orchard with his boyhood gang and throwing them to the pigs has often been thought by later commentators to be overdone (*Confessions*, p. 29). He excoriates himself for his love of rhetoric and his ambition to be a clever orator, for his active sexuality as an adolescent, and even for his love for theater. All is evidence of his sensual enjoyment and love of action, evidence of his restless will. And indeed, he certainly describes his life as frantic and restless. He even condemns himself for falling in love, living faithfully with his beloved for years, and conceiving a son with her. For he acted in "lustful love," rather than entering into the "self-restraint of the marriage-covenant, for the sake of issue" (ibid., book 4, p. 54). Surely that remarkable woman must have profoundly shaped his life and his understanding of love. But she does not fit into his argument, so he denies her formative place in his life. Like many autobiographers, he remembers his life only in its congruence to the point he wishes to make—that sensual enjoyment and love of action keep us from the love of God.

His family of origin is analyzed to make the same point. His mother, Saint Monica, is the heroine of the story. She lives as a faithful Christian, exhorts him to belief and chastity, and hounds him all her life to adherence. I have often thought that if Monica is to be designated *saint* by the tradition, Patricius, his father, should be called long-suffering. For he is the goat in the story. His sins include continuing to want to make love to his wife instead of agreeing to a chaste marriage (ibid., p. 184) and delighting in evidences of his adolescent son's developing sexuality. Even Patricius's financial sacrifices to enable his son's education are only grudgingly mentioned in the context of Patricius's indifference to Augustine's lack of Christian faith (ibid., pp. 27, 26). Evidently, he did beat his wife, although Augustine does not indicate it to be unusual in that period. Patricius is a strong, loving male. But like Augustine's beloved, he does not fit Augustine's argument, and like her is dismissed from his place in the shaping of his son's life.

But the real adversary is not Patricius or Augustine's beloved, but his own restless will which must be pummeled and prayed into submission. In Augustine's own account there is nothing valuable, let alone necessary, in his enjoyment of life, in his developing competence in his profession, or even in the developmental stages through which he must progress to adulthood. With a consistency that seems bizarre, terrifying, and literally unimaginable to a modern American, to Augustine it is all dross. What we might think the best in him—his love for the nameless woman; his restless, inquiring mind; his love of pleasure; his capacity for deep friendship—is for Augustine the worst in him. For all of it is evidence of sensual enjoyment and love of action, and neither has any place in the Christian life. Both are the restless will turning away from love of God. Only in one place in the *Confessions* does he seem to wistfully question his rejection of his own humanity, thus defined. He is speaking of his and his childhood friends' incorrigible desire to play. "But our sole delight was play; and for this we were punished by those who yet themselves were doing the like. But elder folks' idleness is called 'business'; that of boys, being really the same, is punished by those elders; and none commiserates either boys or men" (book 1, p. 12).

There is a profound sadness from the alien perspective of so many centuries that the magnificent vision of the love and praise of God, Augustine's gift to the church, can be realized only through the terrible denial of one's humanity. The profound insight that God is to be seen through the creatures is taken to mean that one must deny the pleasurable seeing of the creatures and acting in relation to them in order to see the images as images. Sometimes the strategies for doing so have a beauty and serenity about them, but always they exact a high price.

Augustine was ordained priest directly from his life as a layman and was consecrated bishop from his activities as a priest. In that sense Augustine's life was still faithful to the New Testament precedent.

Jesus did not send his disciples to seminary, and
neither did the bishop of Hippo before ordaining
Augustine. The institutional applications of Augustine's paradigm are essentially variations of the
monastic disciplines enunciated by Saint Benedict.
The threefold vows of poverty, chastity, and obedience are the church's time-honored strategies for
turning the restless will away from sensual enjoyment and the love of action. Augustine regretted that
his mother had only brought him up as a catechumen
and had not baptized him. Following the wisdom of
the time, she delayed baptism to decrease the
possibility of his sinning after baptism, and so falling
beyond the possibility of redemption. Deathbed
baptisms were common to prevent that occurrence.
However, the church often used the alternate
strategy of beginning the life of denial as early as
possible to prevent the love of things of the world
from taking root, as in the development of adolescent
sexuality. Hence, admission to monastic communities often took place at the beginning of adolescence.

Communities of monastic disciplines at their best
were centers of learning and civilizing influences
wherever Christianity spread. They were the result of
a heroic commitment to live a life solely dedicated to
God, eschewing the worldly ambitions and material
and sensual pleaures that distracted and entrapped
others. They preserved, tested, and passed on a rich
heritage of wisdom in how to live a godly life,
beginning with the desert fathers and continuing
until today. Monastic writers still dominate contemporary literature on spiritual formation. Monasteries
intended to be a holy counterculture, an alternative
community to the culture of the time.

Poverty, chastity, and obedience tightly structured
and carefully prescribed the arena of willing and

loving. They removed most of the choices or decisions by which persons will to love in the world and tightly circumscribed the rest. The moral virtues of prudence, temperance, fortitude, and justice and the theological virtues of faith, hope, and charity were available as abstract guidelines for the choices that did remain, usually about detailed matters of communal living and the restricted interpersonal transactions that accompanied it. As it worked out, verbal exhortation was the main teaching device for training the will. Self-examination, examination by confessors, and spiritual direction refined and confined the will and the person. The effect of these strategies was sometimes the growth of saints and wise old contemplatives. Often, however, they resulted in a privatistic, narcissistic preoccupation with the subleties of interior prayer. As Thomas Merton noted, "The whole trouble comes from the inordinate reflection upon self that is generated by the consciousness of 'degrees of prayer' and steps on the ascent of the 'mountain of love'!" (*Spiritual Direction and Meditation* [Collegeville, Minn.: The Liturgical Press, 1960], p. 32). In some other cases, according to Merton, the despairing penitent prayed only for the power to endure the humiliation and restriction, and the grace of an early death.

# CHAPTER THREE

# Calvin: Can We Know God?

Edward Farley points out that the term *theology, or theologia*, has "had two fundamentally different" meanings as used in the Christian tradition. The first meaning is to experience God. In this first sense theology is a habit (*habitus*) of the human soul (*Theologia: The Fragmentation and Unity of Theological Education* [Philadelphia: Fortress Press, 1983], p. 31). It is a function of faith, a disposition of the soul to be in the presence of God, with eternal happiness as its final aim. Augustine's understanding of faith, to love God instead of the things of this world, was precisely such a *habitus* or disposition of the soul. *Theologia* for Augustine and the monastics had to do with loving God.

The second, very different meaning of theology is

an academic discipline, "a self-conscious scholarly enterprise of understanding" (ibid). In this second sense *theologia* has to do with knowledge about God rather than being in the presence of God; it is content, not experience. Farley has described the history of the emergence and final dominance of this second meaning of *theologia* in the history of theological education. I cannot adequately summarize that fascinating and complex history here. Key points have to do with the emergence of the universities in the Middle Ages and their appropriation of *theologia* as "*scientia* in the distinctive scholastic sense of a method of demonstrating conclusions" (ibid., p. 34). The Protestant Reformation falls within this period from the twelfth century to the Enlightenment and the modern university and shares, along with the Roman Catholic tradition, the developing under-standing of theology as a theoretical science.

Influenced by the thought of Thomas Aquinas and the rediscovery of Aristotle during this period, theology, even in the first sense of experience, is a cognitive state, a knowing of God. In the Aristotelian anthropology, *episteme*, or knowledge, is a "*hexis*, one of the three states or enduring characteristics of the soul." *Hexis* is translated into the Latin *habitus*. Thelogy is a *habitus*, "a cognitive disposition and orientation of the soul, a knowledge of God and what God reveals" (ibid., p. 35). It is more precisely a practical habit, having the characteristic of wisdom. Within this new emphasis upon knowing God, the followers of Augustine continue to insist on the longing of the soul for God and centrality of prayer and grace, and they fight against the dominant understanding of theology as an academic discipline. But the dominant strain, according to Gustavo Gutierrez, agrees with Aquinas, that theology as "the demands of rational knowledge will be reduced to the need for systematization and clear exposition" (*Theology of Liberation* [Maryknoll, N.Y.: Orbis Books, 1973], p.6). This trend continues in the Roman Catholic Church after the Reformation. Scholastic theology after the Council of Trent becomes an ancillary discipline of the magisterium of the church with the following purposes:

    1—to define, present and explain revealed truths
    2—to examine doctrine, to denounce and condemn false
       docrines, and
    3—to teach revealed truths authoritatively. (Ibid., p. 62)

On the Protestant side, theology as scholarly discipline and science was also dominant. Even the Pietists, who most emphasized personal growth in prayer and faith, ironically contributed to this development. They insisted upon prayer and spiritual discipline in theological study. They were keenly opposed to the idea of the minister as a scholar and wished to reclaim the centrality of the experience of the presence of God for those who ministered to others. But ironically, because of this very emphasis, according to Farley, "they very much stressed preparation and training for specific tasks of ministry" (Farley, *Theologia*, p. 41). This emphasis on skill training for ministry overshadowed personal faith experience and led to the fragmentation of *theologia* into specialized theological sciences, each dealing with a particular area of knowledge and skill deemed necessary for effective ministry. It also anticipated the third metaphor for God's call to ministry described in the next chapter.

The second great metaphor for discipling is perhaps most clearly shown in the thought of John Calvin, for whom the central question of the religious life is an elaboration of the concern, "Can we know God?" The term *knowing* has a particular sense about it as Calvin used it. Although he quotes Augustine repeatedly and with approval, Calvin's knowing is not a beatific vision. It is conceptual understanding, made possible by God's sovereign grace. Calvin's knowing owes more to hearing than to seeing. It is saving knowledge, a chain of logical argument. When God enables a person to hear it in faith, it compels to commitment and obedience. It is the audited, authoritative word spoken by the sovereign Lord to his submissive subjects and known to us through the written word of scripture.

The announced purpose of the *Institutes of the Christian Religion* is to explicate "the knowledge of God, as the way to attain a blessed immortality; and in connection with and subservient to this, Secondly, to the knowledge of ourselves" (John Calvin, *Institutes of the Christian Religion*, trans. John Allen, 2 vols. [Philadelphia: Presbyterian Board of Christian Education, 1936], 1:41). The knowledge of God, the primary aim of the *Institutes*, is not a matter of unaided human reasoning. It begins with "his written word" in scripture (ibid.). Indeed, it is not possible to discover it otherwise, for the knowledge of God must be sought,

> 1—Not in man; because, though the human mind is naturally endowed with it, yet it is extinguished, partly by ignorance, partly by wickedness.
> 2—Nor in the structure of the world; because, though it shine there with the brightest evidence, testimonies of that kind, however plain, are, through our stupidity wholly useless to us." (Ibid., 1:45)

Having set his course in this exacting way, Calvin continues with careful and dogged argument for over sixteen hundred pages on salvation as the knowledge of God, choosing scripture which agrees with his focus, e. g., "This is life eternal, to know thee, the only true God, and Jesus Christ, whom thou hast sent" (ibid., 1:368). There are two kinds of knowledge of God. The first, which is not the saving knowledge, is the "simple knowledge, to which the genuine order of nature would lead us, if Adam had retained his innocence." We could, if it were not for the "present ruined state of human nature," understand God as Creator, that he "supports us by his power, governs us by his providence, nourishes us by his goodness, and follows us with blessings of every kind" (ibid., 1:51).

The second, and saving knowledge, is that by which persons, "lost and condemned in themselves, apprehend God the Redeemer in Christ the mediator" (ibid.). Specifically, they understand that "by the sacrifice of Christ we obtain gratuitous righteousness, so as to be acceptable to God, though by nature we are the children of wrath, and alienated from him by sin" (ibid., 1:580).

Calvin writes at great length about our inability to have this saving knowledge of Christ through our unaided human reason:

Some perhaps grow vain in their own superstitions, while others revolt from God with intentional wickedness; but all degenerate from the true knowledge of him. The fact is, that no genuine piety remains in the world. But, in saying that some fall into superstition through error, I would not insinuate that their ignorance excuses them from guilt; because their blindness is always connected with pride, vanity, and contumacy. Pride and vanity are discovered, when miserable men, in seeking after God, rise not, as they ought, above their own level, but judge of him according to their carnal stupidity, and leave the proper path of investigation in pursuit of

speculations as vain as they are curious. Their concep-
tions of him are formed, not according to the representa-
tions he gives of himself, but by the inventions of their
own presumptuous imaginations. (Ibid., 1:58)

It is tempting to pile up quote after quote of
Calvin's grim insistence on human stupidity and
depravity. We are doubly lost, first by ignorance and
then further blinded by sin. Calvin's own fascination
with human wickedness draws us in. His own dark
integrity will not let him turn aside from human
greed, folly, and perversion. It is like a closed tent at a
state fair promising for a small fee a glimpse of some
horrible monster inside. Calvin holds that we are
monsters and draws us within to see it. Here is no
benign Augustinian view that evil is abandoning
better things for lesser things. That monster is not
some small or peripheral aspect of ourselves. It *is we*,
totally. With finely drawn portraits of human
wickedness, Calvin titillates our thrilling dread that
this is what, honestly, we *really* are:

> For we are all so blinded and fascinated with self-love,
> that every one imagines he has a just right to exalt himself,
> and to undervalue all others who stand in competition
> with him. . . . The vices in which we abound, we
> sedulously conceal from others, and flatter ourselves with
> the pretense that they are diminutive and trivial, and even
> sometimes embrace them as virtues. If the same talents
> which we admire in ourselves, or even superior ones,
> appear in others, in order that we may not be obliged to
> acknowledge their superiority, we depreciate and dimin-
> ish them with the utmost malignity: if they have any vices,
> not content to notice them with severe and sharp
> animadversions, we odiously amplify them. Hence that
> insolence, that every one of us, as if exempted from the
> common lot, is desirous of preeminence above the rest of
> mankind; and severely and haughtily condemns every
> man, or at least despises him as an inferior. (Ibid., 1:755)

It not only fascinates us; Calvin believes it conducive to our own best interests and to God's glory, to focus on not just the worst in us, but that the worst in us *is* our essential nature. For to ascribe strength, virtue, or wisdom to ourselves is surely to attempt to diminish God as the sole source of goodness (ibid., 1:280). And then God is our enemy, and justly so. But the more we realize our wretchedness, the more we may be willing to hear this message:

> That in this situation, Christ interposed as an intercessor; that he has taken upon himself and suffered the punishment by which the righteous judgment of God impended over all sinners; that by his blood he has expiated those crimes which render them odious to God; that by this expiation God the Father has been satisfied and duly atoned; that by this intercessor his wrath has been appeased; that this is the foundation of peace between God and men; that this is the bond of his benevolence towards them. (Ibid., 1:553)

That is the good news and our only hope for salvation in the words Calvin commends it to be preached. The good news, however, is not for all who might wish to hear it. Since it is entirely from God and depends in no way upon our own virtue, even the virtue of our desire to be saved, it must, in Calvin's view, be given freely to some and withheld from others. God's glory is shown in his saving some and damning others. To hold otherwise is to diminish our own humility. "We shall never be clearly convinced as we ought to be, that our salvation flows from the fountain of God's free mercy, till we are acquainted with his eternal election, which illustrates the grace of God by this comparison, that he adopts not all promiscuously to the hope of salvation, but gives to some what he refuses to others" (ibid., 2:170-71).

And thus we see Calvin's other preoccupation—the maintenance of God's glory and sovereign power and authority. God must be perfect, as humans are depraved. God must be all powerful and demanding in his authority, as we must be submissive and unable to help ourselves. This is Calvin's religious concern—to maintain the majesty and glory of God. He comes back to the point again and again. The argument he most often uses to uphold his theological conclusions is that they glorify God more effectively than do the alternatives. The remarkable statement just quoted, that the free mercy of God is clearly shown by his arbitrarily damning persons to hell regardless of their prayers or the quality of their life, is merely one example. We must not question God or his authority over us. Our sole intent should be "resigning ourselves and all that we have to the will of God, we should surrender to him the affections of our heart, to be conquered and reduced to subjection" (ibid., 1:760). In this way we "maintain the glory of the Lord unimpaired and undiminished" (ibid., 1:832).

Then this is the saving knowledge of God in Christ, arbitrarily bestowed upon some. For those lucky ones, the Christian life proceeds as follows: they "ought to prepare themselves for a life, hard, laborious, unquiet and replete with numerous and various calamities. It is the will of their heavenly Father to exercise them in this manner, that he may have a certain proof of those that belong to him. Having begun with Christ his first begotten Son, he pursues this method towards all his children" (ibid., 1:76). In other words, why should you have it better than Jesus, who was crucified? The saints are to live a life of self-denial, including bearing a cross when so ordered. Calvin does include a treatise on prayer. Given the context already outlined, it should be clear that prayer doesn't do anything for God. It certainly doesn't give him any new information. But it does help prevent our faith from becoming languid and torpid. Hence four rules for praying, which in another context might be quite helpful:

—our heart and mind be composed to a suitable frame . . .

—join with the petitions themselves a serious and ardent desire of obtaining them . . .

—relinquish all confidence in himself, giving by this humiliation of himself, all the glory entirely to God . . .

—thus prostrate with true humility, we should nevertheless be animated to pray by the certain hope of obtaining our requests. (Ibid., 2:95-107)

After treating the Christian life, Calvin explicitly addresses the issue of ministry. For him ministry is now a public office of the church. The variety of gifts Paul named in the New Testament were only for that time. What remains for us is the office of pastors, who resemble the apostles and whose primary responsibilities are the preaching of the gospel and the administration of the sacraments. The government of the church is committed to the "senate or council, composed of pious, grave, and holy men, who were invested with that jurisdiction in the correction of vices" (ibid., 2:324-25). Deacons have responsibility for the care of the poor. There are also to be teachers, who do not have governmental or sacramental responsibilities and resemble the ancient prophets (ibid., 2:302-21). The office of pastor is now a public office in the church, to be publicly elected, on the

model of the disciples casting lots after the resurrection to replace Judas. Public election, under the
oversight of pastors and carried out with the utmost
reverence through fasting and prayer, constitutes the
call to ministry. The call in the public order of the
church is essential to ministry. There is also the
secret call, whereby a person affirms to himself or
herself, from a sincere fear of God, an ardent zeal for
the edification of the church. But that secret call is
not known to the church, nor essential to the call to
ministry. Indeed, "he who enters on his office with an
evil conscience, is nevertheless duly called, providing
his iniquity be not discovered" (ibid., 2:326).

To be qualified for ministry, persons are to be "of
sound doctrine and a holy life, not chargeable with
any fault that may destroy their authority, or
disgrace their ministry." More specifically, the gifts
mentioned in Corinthians and learning connected
with piety are essential to ministry and constitute a
kind of preparation for it (ibid., 2:327).

Here then, in outline, is Calvin's theological
response to the question of salvation and of call to
ministry. For him the sovereign God of absolute
authority replaces the Eternal and Compassionate
One of Augustine. The problem is human reason
blinded by ignorance and sin instead of the restless
will loving the things of this world rather than God.
This fundamental difference in the problematic
creates informal and formal contrasts with the
thought of Augustine. For example, it is as unthinkable for Calvin to leave us with a confession as it was
natural for Augustine to do so. We come to love
Augustine as he shares with us his own struggles to
love. Calvin does not even invite us to know him, let
alone love him. He is opaque to us in a different way
from Augustine. We marvel at him as at a champion

long-distance runner or a freak in a circus. We are not sure whether to be in awe of his incredible will and ruthless honesty or simply dismayed at his depression. If he came to us for pastoral counseling, we would be most concerned for him. But then, of course, he never would, even if the centuries could be magically spanned.

Knowing as the way to God is very different in the hands of Calvin from loving according to Augustine. Calvin is as careful to keep God from interacting with us as he was to keep Calvin from interacting with us. For to do so would mean in some sense that we had something in common with God, some goodness or wisdom or choice as the basis for interaction. And that, according to Calvin, would diminish God. So our only possibility is to be a passive subject to God the Sovereign Lord, which is a way to avoid interaction. Masters give orders, slaves obey; that is their only official relationship. Knowing means understanding and reverencing the impersonal, already accomplished sacrifice of God in Christ. Knowing God does not mean to be close to or have a personal relationship with God. Those modern, subjective terms are bizarre in this context.

Knowing becomes objective. What we are to do is to understand the chain of biblical argument about Christ's accomplished sacrifice for the whole world. Knowing becomes impersonal. If God chooses us, it has nothing to do with us, but only with his own majesty and goodness. It is passive. We do not even decide to know; God arbitrarily decided that we are to know. It is static. There is nothing new to know; all has been done for salvation. This objective, impersonal, passive, and static knowing becomes knowledge. It becomes a thing, not an event. It becomes the saving knowledge of God in the sacrifice of Christ which God may or may not enable us to know.

This static, perfect knowledge, then, is our authority. Calvin builds his church upon it and quotes from scripture to establish the church's structure and official roles. It is like a magic disappearing act. Augustine the lover, contending with his restless will, facing the abyss, in speechless awe before God the lover, is gone. His concerns are irrevelant to the official life of the church, its authoritative knowledge of dogma, and its public order. To be precise, they are consigned to the arena of the secret call. There one may still contend with the fear and love of God. But it has nothing to do with ministry. Unless, of course, the inner struggle disrupts the public order of the church.

The Enlightenment and the modern university provided a context for establishing the metaphor of knowing God in ministerial education programs. In the university the metaphor to know God is implemented with the teaching of *theologia*, defined as a "way of metaphysics or a systematic ordering and interrelating of the authority-provided themes of scripture" (Association of Thelogical Schools: *Theological Education Quarterly* [Spring 1981], p. 101). *Theologia*, founded on the church's dogmatic authority, was taught as content. It was knowledge, ideas, and facts to be learned as students and taught as pastors. Under the influence of Pietistic concern for trained pastors and Enlightenment ideals of autonomous scholarship, *theologia* was divided in the Germany university into the fourfold division of Bible, church history, dogmatics, and practical theology (ibid., p. 97). Backed by the church's authority and given coherence by the scholarly ordering and integration of the material, the fourfold content effectively prepared ministers for their authoritative teaching ministry in their churches. For they could understand their task as the public instruction of the congregation in the saving knowledge.

This metaphor of theological education also was remarkably sturdy in equipping generations of ministers. Logical argument and commitment to truth at its best formed pastors who were intellectually alive and responsible in their preaching and teaching. Academic disciplines upheld the intellectual integrity of dogma and forced it to encounter new ideas from the culture and emerging scientific disciplines. It might be a murky and problematic task to form and evaluate a seminarian's spiritual growth, but one could be called to intellectual excellence and evaluated by public standards of achievement.

Two developments made the implementation of this approach to formation for ministry problematic. The first was the decline of dogmatic authority. Scholars could no longer so confidently teach by the authority of the church. What then was the warrant for their ideas? Related to this development was the application of historical critical methods of interpretation to scripture. Treating the word of God as a human document to be analyzed by the new method of the secular criticism of history further eroded the claim that it was saving knowledge that was taught (ibid., p. 97).

In their concern, scholars searched the secular knowledge of the time even more for connections to theological disciplines and to ministry. With the loss of the authoritative ordering of the curriculum, the subject matter for theological education became fragmented by the latest enthusiasm for related secular disciplines and by the attempt to address the skills needed for the pastor's role performance.

Farley comments that by the ninteenth century "these connections (among the disciplines) are established not as aspects of a single cognitive endeavor, *Theologia*, but by the concept of the minister and the competencies needed" (*Theologia*, p. 98).

In this country the early nineteenth century was a time of major change in formation for ministry because of the founding of the first denominational seminary in Andover, Massachusetts, followed by Princeton Seminary a decade later. Their founders soon looked to the German university as their model for what theological education should be. Traveling to Germany, they discovered with amazement that individual German scholars had personal libraries in their homes bigger than the whole seminary library back in Princeton. They returned, determined to establish their institutions and programs after the German model. And so the fourfold division of Bible, church history, dogmatics, and practical theology became determinative for education for ministry in this country as well—as did the continuing proliferation and fragmentation of the curriculum to accommodate secular disciplines and methods.

The Auburn project on the history of American theological education has noted the following problems in the contemporary American implementation of this metaphor of education for ministry:

—fragmentation and lack of coherence in the curriculum

—the loss of *Theologia* as a "way of metaphysics or a systematic ordering and interrelating of the authority—founded themes of scripture"

—the irrelevance of academic theology to the real needs of ministers and churches. (*Theological Educational Quarterly*, p. 100-102)

The problem is usually stated in our time as the gap between academic and practical theology. Attempts to bridge the gap in order to meet the needs of ministers and churches usually result in:

—Being captured by "the student's agenda (with) little or no function in criticizing, modifying, or expanding that agenda"

—preoccupation with the technique although "*praxis* occurs not as the result of bridging techniques but in the mysteries of freedom and grace"

—theological disciplines being captured by secular sciences

—new paradigms being kept out of theological education, e.g., "the feminist perspective in theology, liberation theology, black religion and black theology, the new ecological consciousness." (Ibid., pp. 105-8)

# CHAPTER FOUR

# Dewey: Can We Do Ministry?

It is a further leap in the world view even than in centuries from Calvin to the next metaphor for God's call to ministry. The remarkable triumphs of early science made it, rather than organized religion, the authoritative source of statements about the nature of reality. Tenet after tenet of religion crumbled before new, confident assertions by scientists as to what the world and human beings really were like. Religionists began a continuing retreat to territory in which they could continue to be the experts on the nature of things. After the publication of *The Origin of Species* and consequent suggestions that human beings are descended from apes, the wife of the bishop of Chichester was heard to remark that she hoped it were not true, and that if it were, it would not become generally known.

It was not just that scientific findings contradicted religious beliefs, i. e., that the universe by geological evidence was much older than 4004 B.C. The real blow to religious authority came from the fact that the scientific method which was so fruitful in producing these troubling findings was inherently inhospitable to religious concerns. Galileo and his fellow physicists attacked the church's claim to be the sole arbiter of the nature of reality by discovering the difference between *why* questions and *how* questions. There is no empirically verifiable answer to the *why* questions with which traditional religion abounds. Why is there a rainbow? Because God put it there after the flood as a sign to Noah. You either believe that or you don't, but there is no way to discover which alternative is true. But how about the question, *how* does the rainbow happen? Ah, there is a question an empiricist can sink her teeth into. One can study the refraction of white light in water vapor and actually explain how rainbows happen, even create a rainbow on demand by instructions that anyone properly trained and with proper equipment can duplicate. There is an answer to that question and commonly agreed upon criteria to evaluate it against its alternatives. The rise of modern science and the delights and dangers of modern technology resulted from the excitement of *how* questions. This seemed to leave religion with only the *why* questions. And since there was no way to distinguish between truth and illusion in *why* questions, religion seemed unimportant and irrelevant. When the French astronomer and mathematician Pierre Simon LaPlace, following Newton's theories, wrote and presented Napoleon with his multivolume work, the emperor remarked,

"I see you have written this large book on the nature of the universe and have not mentioned God." To which LaPlace replied, "I had no need for that hypothesis" (Fritjof Capra, *The Tao of Physics* [Berkeley: Shambala, 1975], p. 58).

Even when the scientists were believers, they were hard pressed to keep a central place for God in the new world of their discoveries. Sir Isaac Newton wrote as many words of theology as he did of physics, attempting to see his new view of reality as religious vision:

> It seems probable to me that God in the beginning formed matter in solid massy, hard, inpenetrable, movable particles, of such sizes and figures, and with such other properties, and in such proportion to space, as most conduced to the end for which he formed them; and that these primitive particles, being solid, are incomparably harder than any porous bodies compounded of them, even so very hard, as never to wear or break in pieces. (Ibid.)

This revision of the Genesis creation story loses something as religious vision in the translation. The rest of the Newtonian picture of reality is equally dismal from the standpoint of the biblical vision. Those hard (probably black) particles moved in absolute empty space, determined by mathematical laws. The movement was mechanistic and totally determined. LaPlace bragged:

> An intellect which at a given instant knew all the forces acting in nature, and the position of all things of which the world consists—supposing the said intellect were vast enough to subject these data to analysis—would embrace in the same formula the motions of the greatest bodies in the universe and those of the slightest atoms; nothing would be uncertain for it, and the future, like the past, would be present to its eyes. (Ibid., p. 57)

The fundamental division between the I and the world posited by Descartes made this mechanistic determinism possible. It was believed that the world could be described objectively without reference to any human observer, and to do so became the ideal of science.

How could theology express the gospel in such a world? Only by extreme accommodation. God became the great watchmaker in the sky, who wound up the machine in the beginning but obviously would not interfere with the mathematical laws he himself established, except perhaps in extreme emergency. The qualities of being human we prize most highly were equally irrelevant to the working of the cosmic machine. Consciousness was an epiphenomenon—it only seemed to exist, but it made no difference. Love, will, the mystic vision of the connectedness of all reality—they all were relegated to the sphere of private, "subjective" experience. We might entertain ourselves with them, but they were illusory—not *real* like those hard particles. Perhaps most poignant of all, the religious life itself was irrelevant. What possible reason could there be to pray in a universe like that? For self-improvement, perhaps, as long as one didn't think anything changed in reality, outside of one's own thoughts and emotions.

People, of course, continue to believe in God in twentieth-century America. But in an increasingly secularized society, religion is compartmentalized in the sphere of personal, private, and subjective experience. God is no longer the context in which humans live, move, and have their being. It seems to me that the most recent metaphor for God's call to ministry ironically no longer has *God* as its major term. The person who best articulates it was not a believer in traditional terms and had no direct personal participation in the life of the church or in theological education. His influence is indirect, as he has influenced education generally. I would suggest that this latest metaphor be articulated, "Can we do ministry?" and that the person best articulating the theory underlying it is John Dewey.

Dewey stands in the heritage of pragmatism, that distinctly American philosophical tradition. Pragmatism, as developed by C. S. Peirce and others, holds that thinking is a practical matter. Specifically, one must "refer to *consequences* for the final meaning and test of all thinking" (John Dewey, *On Experience, Nature, and Freedom* [New York: Bobbs-Merrill, 1960], p. xv). One thinks in order to achieve some interest or end, and the meaning of the thinking lies in those consequences. For Dewey, one thinks when one is in what he called a "forked-road situation." One has a choice to make, and the thinking is for the purpose of solving the problem or impasse the environment presents in order that a choice can be made (*John Dewey: His Thought and Influence*, ed. John Blewett, S. J. [New York: Fordham University Press, 1960], pp. 68-69).

Thinking is thus a very active enterprise, not the passive beholding of Augustine or Calvin's submissive reception of knowledge. It is not separate from willing, but united with it; and the willing directs the knowing. "There is no knowledge of anything except as our interests are alive to the matter, and our will actively directed toward the end desired. We know only what we most *want* to know" (Blewett, *Thought and Influence*, p. 60).

Dewey understands thinking biologically; it is a matter of the organism adapting to its environment. Knowledge, therefore, the result of the activity of knowing, derives from "the interaction of organism and environment, resulting in some adaptation which secures utilization of the latter." Knowing is like shaping or making something. It is "an act which confers upon non-cognitive material traits which *did* not belong to it" (ibid., pp. 72, 74).

Dewey is especially impatient with the usual dualism between subject and object, or the knower and the known. His early interest in Hegel enabled him to overcome his personal and "painful sense of divisions and separations," that was, he believed, "a consequence of a heritage of New England culture, divisions by way of isolation of self from the world, of soul from body, of nature from God." He came to replace Hegel's synthesis of subject and object with an organic understanding of the interrelatedness of organism and environment, thus continuing his opposition to the dualism of subject and object. "There is but one world, the world of knowledge, not two, an inner and an outer, a world of observation and a world of conception; and this one world is everywhere logical" (ibid., pp. 60-61).

Dewey's model for knowing comes from the development of scientific method, especially as related to problem solving. Knowledge is the "outcome of competent and controlled inquiry" (ibid., p. 76). He lists specific logical steps in the process, having to do with the general movement from (1) the antecedent or given situation, to (2) defining and limiting the situation according to one's interests, to (3) the object of inquiry itself (ibid., p. 75). One list of "reflective experiences" gives the following steps:

—a felt difficulty
—its location and definition
—suggestion of possible solution

—development by reasoning of the bearings of the
   suggestions
—further observation and experiment leading to its
   acceptance or rejection; that is, the conclusion of belief
   or disbelief.
     (Dewey, *Experience, Nature and Freedom,* p. xxvii)

Knowing, then, is "literally something we do."
Specifically, he views it as an art and approves the
earlier days when *art* and *science* were virtually
equivalent terms, when the "divorce of knowledge
and action, theory and practice had not been
decreed." This does not mean that the consequences
of thinking have only to do with physical survival
concerns. They may be aesthetic, moral, political, or
religious. In fact, as will be evident below, he is
particularly concerned with applying scientific
methods of knowing into what he calls morals
(Blewett, *Thought and Influence,* p. 73).

Knowing (the process) and knowledge (the prod-
uct) are not really separable. Knowledge (i. e., what I
know) and knowing (how I came to the knowledge)
are aspects of one reality. Each must be understood
in order to understand the other. Knowing is a
dynamic interaction with one's environment, not a
static copy of external reality. Dewey writes against
the "kodak fixation" which separates knowledge
from knowing and regards it as a static and exact
copy of reality (ibid., p. 71).

He is concerned to apply the power of the scientific
method to matters of the social life as well. In his
introduction to the new edition of *Reconstruction in
Philosophy,* written twenty-five years after the original, Dewey expresses his concern to "carry over into
any inquiry into human and moral subjects the kind
of method (the method of observation, theory as
hypothesis, and experimental test) by which under-

standing of physical nature has been brought to its
present pitch" (John Dewey, *Reconstruction in
Philosophy* [New York: H. Holt & Co., 1920], p. ix). He
believes that valuing can be subject to scientific
judgment (Dewey, *Experience, Nature and Freedom*,
p. xxxiii) and that great benefits to humankind would
result from using his theory of knowing in the field of
morals. Logic should connect morals and science
(Blewett, *Thought and Influence*, p. 88).

This application of scientific method to morals
does not involve abstracting the method from its
rootedness in physical reality. According to Dewey,
nothing can be said to be known which is "not
operable by the knower," i. e., not acted upon in the
inquiry (ibid., p. 78). All knowledge is practical
knowledge, with its consequences in the interaction
of organism and environment, in morals as well as in
physical science.

And thus we come to the place of religion in
Dewey's thought. In the Terry lectures at Yale,
published as *A Common Faith* (New Haven: Yale
University Press, 1970), he insists that religious
sentiment or attitude still has an important place in
his program for the improvement of humankind. This
is so because ideals such as justice are powerful
realities in human lives, motivating persons to
action. In addition, the self is purposive and requires
some ideal end to integrate and make sense of its
strivings. "The self is always directed toward
something beyond itself and so its own unification
depends upon the idea of the integration of the
shifting scenes of the world into that imaginative
totality we call the universe" (p. 19).

God in Dewey's view, then, can "denote the unity of
all ideal ends arousing us to desire and action." If we
would just free religion from its "apparatus of dogma

and doctrine," we could enhance the power of ideal ends operating in human lives, arousing us to action to realize them. If that could happen, "religion would then be found to have its natural place in every aspect of human experience that is conceived with estimate of possibilities, with emotional stir by possibilities as yet unrealized, and with all action in behalf of their realization. All that is significant in human experience falls within this frame" (ibid., pp. 42, 57).

Dewey spent much of his career developing and applying his theories in relation to education. Given his pragmatic orientation, it is understandable that he was very critical of the educational methods of his day and set about to conceptualize and to demonstrate alternatives. He even had great difficulty finding desks that would enable children to actively do/think, instead of sitting passively. The great principle for him in education, proclaimed in his Pedagogic Creed, was that "education is a process of living and not a preparation for future living." Education is a "continuing reconstruction of experience; that the process and goal of education are one and the same thing" (Blewett, *Thought and Influence*, pp. 95-96). If children are not passively preparing to live life at some future time, but living and learning to live more effectively at the same time in the present, then the emphasis on education should be on "the concrete, the empirical and the practical" (ibid., p. 89).

The social organization in which education should take place is democracy. For democracy is the application of effective method of inquiry to morals. It is the scientific method used to live together and to make judgments of value. Democracy is more than a form of government. It is a "mode of associated living, of conjoint communicated experience," based

on the application of the scientific method for the
satisfaction of human needs (ibid.). Children ought to
be socialized by participating in democratic processes. Such participation not only teaches the social
aims and adult roles of their culture, it teaches them
how to go about moral inquiry in the process.

Dewey's ideas about knowing and about education
seem to me to articulate the theory underlying the
metaphor I have characterized by the question, "Can
we do ministry?" That metaphor is expressed in
programs and types of contemporary rhetoric about
change in theological education. The gap between
academic and practical theology in seminary education noted by Farley has been long felt, especially by
graduates of seminaries who find themselves ill
prepared for the actual life of the parish ministry.
The interest in understanding thelogical education as
professional education comes from that felt need for
theological education to be more useful and relevant
for parish ministries. Dewey's ideas about knowing
and education make sense out of that need and give a
theoretical base for a different understanding of
theological education from Calvin and the German
university. Whether used explicitly or not, they
undergird the understanding of theological education as professional education. James Glasse in
*Profession: Minister* summarized and popularized the
argument that ministry is a profession like law or
medicine. In fact it is the original profession from
which all others evolved. The minister as professional is one who applies coherent theory to specific
situations of human need, using professional skills
and following a standard of ethics in doing so. The
education needed to become such a professional is
congruent with the kind of education that Dewey
recommended. A number of symposiums have been

held looking at education in other professions, such as medicine, law, business, and education, to ascertain what might be learned for the benefit of theological education. Those professors in seminary who have the responsibilites (according to the German distinction) in practical theology call their professional association the Association for Professional Education for Ministry. The term *education for ministry* is probably theirs more than anyone else's (*Education for Ministry: Theology, Preparedness, Praxis*, Report of the Fifteenth Biennial meeting of the APEM, November 17–19, 1978, Trinity College, Toronto, Canada). The Carnegie Study of Theological Education and its authors H. R. Niebuhr, D. D. Williams, and J. M. Gustafson concluded that theological education is "too much an affair of piecemeal transmission of knowledge and skills" and offers "too little challenge to the student to develop his own resources and to become an independent, lifelong inquirer, growing constantly while he is engaged in the work of ministry." As Dewey said, education is not preparation for living, it is the process of living itself. Professional educators for ministry commend Charles E. Fielding's 1966 study for the American Association of Theological Schools for their prescription. In that study, entitled appropriately *Education for Ministry*, he held that "ministry today is generally discontinuous with the preparation provided for it" and recommended that professional education be understood as "the acquisition of knowledge, the development of professional skill, personal human growth and deepening of Christian commitment" (p. 25).

Ministry as professional competence is illustrated in clinical pastoral education. Anton Boisen was a graduate student at Union Theological Seminary in

New York City and Teachers College of Columbia University in the 1920s. He suffered a schizophrenic break and was hospitalized in Worcester State Hospital in Worcester, Massachusetts. After six weeks of mental confusion, he awoke one morning to see a cross at his window. Even after he came to realize that the cross was formed by the bars on the window, he believed that his schizophrenia had profound religious significance. It constituted a desperate search for meaning which plunged him into depths of pain and confusion, but which also gave profound religious meaning to his life. He came to believe that ministers and psychiatrists ought to work together in addressing emotional problems and mental illness. For psychology and religion together were necessary to understand and treat the person in such distress.

Clinical pastoral education, specific training to effect this integration, soon became institutionalized in various professional associations which in time merged into two: the Association for Clinical Pastoral Education and the American Association of Pastoral Counselors. Clinic pastoral education (CPE) became part of most seminary curricula, and most seminary graduates of the last two decades have spent some time in hospitals under the supervision of certified chaplains, learning the intimate skills of relating to patients on a one-to-one basis. CPE is a central way Dewey's metaphor has made its way into professional theological education. It is an example of practical knowledge with a well formed methodology which is highly valuable in the actual work of ministry. It usually suffers from a secular bias, basing its theory and skills on secular psychology and psychotherapy, and adding on what is called theological reflection.

# CHAPTER FIVE

# The Holoverse

Each of these three great historic metaphors for the healing purpose has made its central contribution to our contemporary understanding of how God calls us to mission and ministry. And each is in some essential way an insufficient metaphor for our time. The evidence for that assessment is in current discussions about reform of theological education, the disgruntled comments of ministers about the inadequacy of their seminary education, and the frustrations of lay persons in finding useful resources to equip them for their ministry in the world.

One example of that dissatisfaction is the so-called gap between academic and what is called practical theology, and the indifference or inability of the former to address central questions in ministry. A seminary professor himself states this problem most sharply in a published discussion about theological education as professional education: "Now, I'm not in practical theology, so I am not so much interested in how you work this decision out, but rather in how you justify it theologically" (*Theological Education as Professional Education* [privately published, Boston: Episcopal Divinity School, 1969], p. 143). Ministers, however, have to "work the decision out"; they have to act faithfully and effectively. They are mightily frustrated by theology which is preoccupied with speculations about and justifications of action instead of action itself. Ordained pastors resent the powerful and implicit presentation of the seminary professor as the role model for ministry. Writing papers and giving lectures about ministry is a poor model for doing ministry. Even further, it is often explicitly suggested that the minister is to be a theologian, defined as one who does critical thelogical reflection. The minister knows better; she has to act, not just to critically reflect on action. Although it is very popular to do so, to call her task one of action-reflection does not help much, for the emphasis in the seminary curriculum is on the reflection, not the action. The problem is not addressed by taking more skill development courses. For the skill development courses are in practical theology, often the second-class area of the curriculum, and not central to the theological education enterprise. One minister reports having become very skilled at pastoral counseling, and finding no relation between it and his self-understanding as a minister.

Another example is the indifference of institutions concerned for ministry with the experience of faith itself. An American Association of Theological Schools study (1972) reports, "In all frankness, we have repeatedly heard the cry of the ministerial student that no one has seemed concerned about the state of his soul, that no one has asked him about his spiritual life" (*Voyage Vision Venture: A Report on Spiritual Development* [Dayton: AATS, 1972], p. 38). In the years since then, the widespread interest in spirituality has increasingly found its way into seminary courses, but the academic study of prayer is not the same as praying. Recent graduates as well as older ministers continue to report their frustration at finding the seminary such a barren place in which to nurture their own spiritual life and to learn to respond to the personal faith crises and concerns of their parishioners. Ministers often do not learn to pray in seminary or to find the deep, sustaining nurture of personal religious disciplines for their ministry.

The institutions and programs concerned with God's call to ministry have had too little to do with the healing of purpose. They have too distantly re-presented Jesus' calling and empowering persons to ministry. They have operated too much on the periphery, teaching valuable knowledge and skills, but not touching persons at the center of their faith and empowering them in ministerial action. Theology since the Middle Ages has become too much discourse in nominalizations rather than invitation to action. A nominalization is a linguistic device that transforms an ongoing process into a static state of being by changing verbs into nouns. Its psychological effect is to change personal ownership and participation into impersonal, passive observation. Jesus' invitations were direct, specific verbs: preach, heal, sell all you have, and give to the poor. Over the centuries those concrete verbs have transmuted into abstract nouns. "Salvation" replaces "take up your bed and walk." Salvation sounds like a static state of being. "Take up your bed and walk" is something I must do. I can impersonally discuss salvation as an abstract idea. I must personally take up my bed or not, but I cannot observe my response from a safe distance.

As theology has become discussion of nominalizations, programs of equipping for ministry have lost their metaphorical likeness to Jesus' discipling. For Augustine, willing to love was still the heart of the matter, but the active will must be quieted, not essentially expressed through action in the world. With Calvin *theologia* becomes saving knowledge passively received by the elect. Theology is now a system of authoritative nominalizations taught to ministers to be passed on to congregations. Dewey in the twentieth century reunites willing, doing, and thinking, but in a secular frame. God gets in the way by existing. Subjective religious sentiment may motivate to action as well as may any other useful attitude.

What is needed is a faithful likeness of Jesus' calling, expressed through a unity of willing, loving, knowing, doing. The massive *Readiness for Ministry* study of the Association of Theological Schools implicitly described the need in its findings. Its extensive interviews of five thousand clergy, laity, and seminary faculty and senior students resulted in sixty-four statistically discovered clusters of attributes of effective and faithful ministry. The sixty-four clusters were further grouped into eleven factors or "dimensions" of ministry. The most important dimension describing effective ministry was named "open, affirming style." The authors go on to define what they mean by the phrase: "It is a dimension of ministry that is more than a 'style', more than 'openness', more than 'affirming', and even more than the impact of the three yoked together. This theme weaves into a common fabric ideas about the functions of ministry and the qualities of style and approach that transcend the function" (*Ministry in America*, ed. David S. Schuller, Merton P. Strommen, and Milo L. Brekke [San Francisco: Harper & Row, 1980], p. 30).

It seems to me that the authors, in reporting and interpreting these empirical findings, are groping toward a description of ministry that does indeed unite willing, loving, knowing, and doing. It cannot be reduced to functional skills on the professional education model as they themselves state. The loving/knowing/doing must participate in and be grounded in the presence of God in Christ, as Urban Holmes states and as the vague word *style* seems to suggest.

We are not the first or only generation to live in apocalyptic times. But the unpredictable possibilities of mass destruction through nuclear war are beyond any precedent since the fourteenth century. One third of the human race between India and Iceland died from the plague in the years from 1348 to 1352. Possible destruction at least as awesome as that faces us now. It is the horrifying, if most often denied, backdrop to any discussion assuming the continuation of life on the planet. Any discussion of other matters seems insignificant in light of it. And yet, metaphors for healing of purpose that can call and empower persons to ministry may be remarkably important in motivating persons out of apathy and denial toward effective action to stop the possible approach of the holocaust.

Farley suggests in the conclusion of his critique of theological education that *theologia* begins with the concrete historical situation in which persons find themselves (Farley, *Theologia*, p. 65). Gutierrez

believes that the theology of the Enlightenment was
written in response to the imagined questions of the
nonbeliever. Such nonbelievers were in fact European bourgeois middle-class devotees of the Enlightenment faith in autonomous reason and the primacy
of the individual. They saw no reason to believe in a
traditional Christian God. Gutierrez proposes theology in response to the questions of the nonperson, the
poor and the dispossessed of the Latin American
situation in which he lives and ministers (*The Power
of the Poor in History* [Maryknoll, N.Y.: Orbis Books,
1983], p. 93). Many Americans are, I believe, both
nonbelievers and on the way to becoming nonpersons. The very liberal theology which accommodated
us to the Enlightenment is irrelevant in the light of a
scientific revolution which renders obsolete the
world view to which liberal theology was trying to
accommodate. The scientific nonbeliever now asks
questions radically different from those in Schleier-
macher's time. And to the extent that we all
unwittingly or wittingly absorb the science of the
time as the arbiter of truth, we are all nonbelievers.

Many Americans are also on the way to becoming
nonpersons. We still like to think of ourselves as
affluent sympathizers with the misfortunes of the
Third World poor. Even when basic industries
abruptly shift their factories to other parts of the
world with cheaper labor costs, we want to believe
the incidents to be unfortunate exceptions, without
significance to the rest of us. We are afraid to even
consider the possibilities of nuclear holocaust, let
alone commit ourselves to sustained action to prevent its occurrence. And we are not even aware of the
complex interactions of multinational corporations
that render us increasingly powerless to affect even
our own lives.

The world is changing, and our self-understanding is changing. God calls us to mission and ministry in the midst of those changes. The historic metaphors for the healing of purpose must be reexamined in the light of those changes. We begin that reexamination by considering how our understanding of the world is changing, and in the next chapter, how our self-understanding is changing. Our understanding of the world is changing through the revolutions of modern science, especially subatomic physics. That may seem a strange place to begin to reexamine metaphors for the healing of purpose. But those metaphors have to do with God. And God has always been understood by means of cultural ideas about the nature of ultimate reality. Augustine, for example, explicitly acknowledges his indebtedness to Neoplatonism for much of his understanding of God. Calling persons to ministry is understood by means of cultural ideas about how to particpate in God's reality. It makes no difference whether or not the arbiters of cultural definitions of reality wish to see explicit connections between their work and theological concerns or not. In an earlier day the point was meaningless because philosophical statements about the nature of ultimate reality explicitly referred to God. Today physicists and brain-mind researchers are articulating dazzling and revolutionary insights about the nature of ultimate reality without any reference to traditional religious language. In this chapter we will explore some of those ideas which characterize the basic reality in which we live as the "holoverse." We need to note that the researchers responsible for these insights often enter disclaimers that their revolutionary work has no wider implications. Physicists, for example, wish to regard "quantum mechanics as merely a set of rules that prescribe the outcome of experiment. According to this view quan-

tum theory is concerned only with observable phenomena (the observed position of the pointer) and not with
any underlying physical state (the real position of the
electron)" (Bernard d'Espagnat, "The Quantum Theory
of Reality," *Scientific American* [November 1979], p.
158). But whether they wish it or not, the implications of
their work for a changing world view will not be
disregarded. Just as the laws of classical physics seeped
down into the common language and thought to
powerfully influence what we call common sense, so
will these newer discoveries. In addition, strictly
empirical findings are never satisfying in themselves.
We want to know their underlying explanation and will
search until we do. The relation between the tides and
the moon was known for many centuries, but they were
not understood until the development of Newton's
theory of universal gravitation (ibid., p. 160).

Theologians and enablers of ministry, then, have
no choice. They are in the business of describing
ultimate reality and how to be in touch with it. And
they must use the best available cultural resources to
do so. Process theologians, by adopting the thought of
Alfred North Whitehead, the first major philosopher
to understand modern physics and the mathematics
on which it is based, are doing just that. If
theologians pretend they are not, and are only
articulating the pure faith without philosophical
elaboration, they are only unconsciously repeating
the cultural assumptions of an earlier age in doing so.

When fundamental cultural beliefs about the
nature of reality shift, metaphors for call to ministry
must also shift, whether or not they consciously
intend to do so. Noticing these cultural shifts, then,
can give important clues to the connection and
differentiation from these early metaphors and the
possibility of a new one.

Modern scientific theories, especially in physics and brain-mind research and increasingly in biology, suggest a remarkably different understanding of reality from that of classical physics and the common-sense view of the world that resulted from it. The congruence between these new emerging world views and central themes of the biblical witness is equally dramatic. I will briefly outline here some current ideas about the nature of reality as background for describing a new metaphor for the healing of purpose based on worship, prayer, and meditation practice.

In very simple terms, the view of reality emerging from subatomic physics and modern astronomy looks like this: Physical reality is not composed of funda-mental building blocks of matter, but of fields of energy which comprise the universe. Subatomic physics, in its search for fundamental building blocks or particles, has found them to disappear and change into mutating patterns of energy best understood through field theory. Matter becomes, then, a tem-porary condensation or density of a field of energy.

The universe is one continuum, which can be called space-time, in which everything is ultimately con-nected with everything else. Modern physics has unified space and time into a single continuum which is relative to the observer, curved by gravity, and which is not separate from "objects" that reside in it. This description of reality is so far removed from the ordinary language of our everyday views of reality that it is difficult to find metaphors and word-pic-tures which can even clumsily describe it.

Consciousness is an integral part of the universe. Modern physics has discovered that the observer interacts with the particles under observation in such a way that one cannot isolate the observer from the observed system in an accurate description of the resulting phenomena or interaction. As Heisenberg noted, "What we observe is not nature itself, but nature exposed to our method of questioning". (Lawrence LeShan, *The Medium, the Mystic, and the Physicist* [New York: Viking Press, 1975]).

Within this picture of the physical universe, there are many promising issues that may be chosen to exemplify their exciting theological implications. For example, the strict determinism of classical physics is replaced by the uncertainty principle discovered by Heisenberg. Scientists reach a certain point in the subatomic realm in which one or another aspect of what they are looking at becomes blurred, and there is no way to clarify that aspect without blurring another one. "There are limits beyond which we cannot measure accurately, at the same time, the processes of nature. These limits are not imposed by the clumsy nature of our measuring devices . . . but rather by the very way that nature presents itself to us" (Gary Zukav, *The Dancing Wu Li Masters* [New York: Bantam Books, 1979]). Uncertainty and perhaps choice seem to be built in to physical reality.

But perhaps the most fruitful entry point is science's agreement with the scriptural witness to the coherence of the creation. In Christ all things were created, and in Christ "all things hold together" (Colossians 1:17b). God notices and cares for even the birds of the air and the grass in the field (Matthew 6:25-33). Modern physics likewise holds that the universe is an interdependent whole in which everything is connected with everything else. In fact the research which suggests this view does it in an extreme way which contradicts our common sense. The research contests the premise of what is called "Einstein separability or Einstein locality, which states that no influence of any kind can propagate faster than the speed of light" (d'Espagnat, "Quantum Theory," p. 158).

Einstein agreed with Newtonian physics and common sense that objects existed separately in specific places or localities; and that they cannot move to another place faster than the speed of light. One object cannot exist in two places at the same time, or send signals faster than the speed of light to another object, or be in some sort of mystical union or participation with another object at a distance.

Recent experimental findings in quantum mechanics demonstrate that this commonsense view is "almost certainly in error" (ibid., p. 158). Or even worse, if one wishes stubbornly to cling to the idea, one must give up one of two even more fundamental assumptions about the nature of reality: that there are objects at all out there apart from the observer, or that one can reason inductively from empirical data.

How did physicists get to this fascinating state of affairs? The experiments involved a characteristic of subatomic particles called their spin, which is analogous only in some respects to the angular momentum of a larger body such as the earth itself. A well established and fascinating property of many subatomic particles is that "no matter what axis is chosen for a measure of a spin component, the result can take on only one of two values," which can be designated plus or minus (ibid., p. 165). Further, when two protons, for example, are brought together in a quantum mechanical configuration called a singlet state, there always a strict negative correlation between the spin of the two particles when the same axis of spin is measured. If particle A is plus, particle B is minus on the same component of spin.

Different components of spin may be measured, but the measurement itself changes the spin. This led experimenters to measure particle A along one axis and particle B along another. If the first of the two particles in the singlet state is plus on axis A, one can infer that the second particle is minus on the same component. If the second particle measures plus on axis B, the first particle will measure minus. Thus one simultaneous measurement of each of the two particles can give information about two components of spin, since one can infer that the same component on the other particle has the opposite value.

No matter how far apart the particles travel from the singlet state, the negative correlation of spin on the same component is found. John S. Bell developed the mathematics that enabled experimenters to deduce the values on all three axes of spin from simultaneous observations on two different components, one for each of the particulars. (Only one measurement could be made on each particular, because the spin itself is altered by the observation, and any second measurement would deal with a different situation.)

The Bell inequality describes the state of affairs that should result when the particles fly apart and exist separately in a specific locality, and cannot somehow influence or communicate with each other faster than the speed of light. Amazingly enough, in experiments using various particles (low-energy photons, high energy photons, and pairs of protons) the Bell inequality does not hold. (The Bell inequality does not hold for five of the seven experiments as of November 1979. Those five involve larger samples of data, and violate it in precisely the way quantum theory predicts [ibid., pp. 173-74]).

What does all this mean? Somehow the pairs of particles, distant as they go from each other, continue to communicate with each other instantaneously (faster than the speed of light) or continue in some fashion to be one, even though they are in two locations. Their behavior demonstrates a continuing linkage or mutual influence that contradicts the commonsense view that they are separate objects in different locations.

A researcher attempts to describe this state of affairs so contradictory to common sense: "Most particles or aggregates of particles that are ordinarily regarded as separate objects have interacted at some time in the past with other objects. The violation of separability seems to imply that in some sense all those objects constitute an indivisible whole" (ibid., p. 181).

Evidently once systems have interacted, they continue to be linked by a mysterious quantum connection. "Once connected, always connected," according to John Bell. The quantum connection is not carried by any known field; "despite their apparent separation, the very beings of the two systems never part." The connection is instantaneous, unmediated, and does not diminish with distance—it is as strong at a million miles as at an inch. Bell concludes that "reality is non-local. The difference between here and there is, on some level, unreal" (Esalen Catalogue [1981], pp. 7-8).

This coherent universe, particularly in light of biological findings, is composed of entities that are both wholes in their own right and parts of a greater whole. From subatomic particles to the biosphere, nothing can be found in nature that is not a whole—that is, coherent and self-assertive and independent to a degree. But neither can anything be found that is not, at the same time, "part of a greater whole—a whole to which it is subordinate" (Anna Lemko, "Of Holism, Freedom, and the Creative Meeting of Opposites," *ReVision* 4, no. 2, p. 80). The interdependence of the universe is expressed through the seemingly infinite relationships of entities acting both in their own right and as parts of greater wholes.

How does the human mind function in this coherent, interdependent universe? Specifically, how does it know reality? Some of the most exciting theorizing has been done by a neuroscientist from Stanford named Karl Pribram. Pribram has been on the forefront of brain research for thirty years, concerned, among other interests, with discovering the location and processes of memory (Marilyn Ferguson, "Karl Pribram's Changing Reality," *ReVision* [Summer–Fall 1978], p. 9). Brain researchers agree in frustration that there is no one site in the brain for memory storage. Pribram, working under Karl Lashhay as a neurosurgeon, trained experimental animals, then selectively removed portions of their brains attempting to find the source of memory. There was no specific source. Short of destroying the whole brain, it was not possible to remove what they had been taught. The question remained for him: How could memory be distributed throughout the whole brain?

In the 1960s Pribram read an article describing the first construction of a hologram, a three-dimensional picture produced by lensless photography. (The first hologram seen in a commercial film was the image of Princess Leia in *Star Wars*.) The image is seen as suspended in space and can be viewed from any angle just as the object it represents. The mathematics for it were worked out in 1947, but the invention of the laser beam was a necessary precondition for its first actual construction in 1965.

The principles making the hologram possible solved Pribram's question about the storage of memory and, as we shall see later, connected with Bell's theorem of the indivisible wholeness of reality. In 1947 Dennis Gabor developed the mathematics that could transform an object into a wave storage pattern, and a wave storage into an image. He called the wave storage pattern a hologram because one of its most interesting characteristics is that information about the object is distributed over the entire surface of the photographic film. Each point of light diffracted from the object becomes blurred and is spread over the whole film in a precise mathematical way called a spread function. Waves move out from each point of light like waves on a pond when a pebble strikes its surface. Waves coming from many points of light crisscross each other like waves on the pond when many pebbles are thrown in. The crossing of the waves sets up patterns of interfering wave fronts on the pond surface. If the surface is suddenly frozen, it becomes a hologram. "The photographic hologram is such a frozen record of interference patterns" (Karl Pribram, "What the Fuss Is All About," *ReVision* [Summer–Fall 1978], p. 67).

To make a hologram, a coherent beam of light, in which the waves are of one frequency (laser), is split in two. One falls directly on the photographic plate; the other is first reflected off the subject and then strikes the plate. The result is the hologram. To the eye it is a meaningless bunch of swirls; but when reconstituted by another laser beam, a three-dimensional image is projected into space.

A fascinating characteristic of the hologram is that any part of it will reconstruct the entire image. If the

piece broken off is very small, the image will lose
detail, but the whole image will be there. Discovering
this characteristic, Pribram considered the possibility that "the distributed memory store of the brain
might resemble this holographic record" (ibid.). As a
result of careful research and model building, he
developed a holographic theory of brain functioning.

The human mind, according to the holographic
model, is able to know on two different levels or in
two dimensions. The first is the level of sensory
reality, often called the Newtonian or Euclidean
order. On this level our phenomenal experience is
pretty much as our senses present it to us. Pribram
points out that our senses work by means of *lenses*,
which focus and objectify our experience. The lens of
the eye focuses and objectifies light rays for us so that
we see a tree as a defined object separate from us. The
cochlea of the ear and the touch sensors also work in a
lens-like way. And so have the theorizing of scientists
and theologians attempting to describe reality as
separate objects or particles of matter existing at
random in empty space.

Sensory knowledge is essential and useful in daily
living. But it is not the only way—indeed not the
primary way—the mind knows. For information is
actually stored in the brain holographically, not
sensorially. Brain cells encode information directly
by means of psychophysiological processes which
can be understood mathematically. The encoded
information has holographic properties. Information
about the whole is stored in each part of the relevant
receptive area. The information is meaningless,
sensorially speaking, until it is transformed mathematically by a Fourier transform into sensory
images. The appropriate mathematical transformation brings order of what seems to be random

distribution of stimulation. The information is stored mathematically, directly, holographically.

The holographic information *does not make sense* because it has not been focused by a sensory lens. It is not only nonsense, it is about nothing/no thing, because it has not been focused by sensory lenses into images of objects. It is perhaps direct information about the universe outside of us and inside before it has been further processed into images. That idea took Pribram a giant step further in his theorizing.

So far, he had developed a very exciting model of the brain which integrates findings from many different areas of research, from memory to studies of perception to altered states of consciousness and psychic phenomena. But being insatiably curious and wide ranging in his interests, he began musing on the next question. Lecturing one night in Minnesota in the early 1970s, he referred to the gestalt psychological concept that external reality and brain processes are similar. He suddenly said, "Maybe the *world* is a hologram" (Ferguson, "Pribram's Changing Reality," p. 11).

That mind bender took him to a week-long conversation with his physicist son and the discovery of the work of David Bohm, an eminent theoretical physicist at the University of London and a follower of Krishnamurti. Bohm, extrapolating from Bell's theorem and related findings with the help of the westernized Hindu teachings of Krishnamurti, was describing a holographic universe. After much further collaboration between the two men, and indeed among a number of thinkers, a model of a holographic universe or holoverse emerged that looks something like the following.

The mathematical wave function described by Gabor in 1947 that made the hologram possible is reciprocal. That is, an object can be transformed into a wave function and the wave function can be transformed into an image. But the process works exactly the same in reverse. An image can be transformed into a wave function and the wave function can be transformed back into an object, mathematically speaking.

Pribram concluded that there are two domains of reality: the holographic wave function or frequency domain and the image/object domain. The frequency domain transforms objects into images. The mind, according to Pribram's theory, is holographic in its functioning: it is in the frequency domain. The process works the other way as well, though we are not used to believing that it does. Carl Simonton has demonstrated the efficacy of mental visualization (image) in actually eliminating cancer cells (object) in the body. Moshe Feldenkrais believes the mental image a person holds of her body powerfully influences the actual functioning of that body in external reality.

By violating Einsteinian locality and separability, external reality demonstrates holographic character-istics of information simultaneously distributed throughout the whole. Therefore, external reality as well as the mind must be constructed similarly in some fundamental way. Specifically they both seem to exist in two domains: the holographic realm and the realm of objects and images sanctioned by Newton and common sense. Pribram writes, "In the holographic domain, each organism represents in some manner the universe within it" (Pribram, "What the Fuss Is," p. 17). Mental operations and the basic order of the universe are both holographic. The physicist Bohm calls the holographic or frequency domain the implicate order of the universe or holoverse and the object/image domain the explicate order of the holoverse.

What is this implicate or fundamental order of the holoverse like? In Genesis God creates light immediately after creating the heavens and the earth, and in the Gospels Christ is the true light that enlightens everyone. Bohm believes that light is a useful way to describe the fundamental nature of the universe according to modern physics.

> From the point of view of present field theory, the fundamental fields are those of very high energy in which mass can be neglected, which would be essentially moving at the speed of light . . . all matter is a condensation of light into patterns moving back and forth at average speeds which are less than the speed of light. ("Of Matter and Meaning: The Super-Implicate Order," a conversation between David Bohm and Renee Weber, *ReVision* 6, no. 1, p. 36)

At light, or to use common language, at the "speed" of light, time slows down and stops. One can go from one end of the universe to the other without growing older. Distance is shortened until it is zero "along" a light ray; there is immediate contact from source to observer. Light then transcends time and space in Euclidean order; and causality as well, which depends upon them. Light, according to Bohm, is "energy, and it is also information, content, form and structure. It is the potential of everything." All the diverse structures of matter can be produced by the interaction of different light rays. It was noted above that the universe is a whole consisting of parts which are entities in their own right and parts of larger wholes. Holographically, information about the whole is in each part. "Light, in its generalized sense (not just ordinary light) is the means by which the entire universe unfolds into itself" (ibid., p. 37).

Light as a descriptor of the fundamental nature of the universe is prior to the Kantian categories by which we grasp sensory reality: time, space, and cause and effect. The implicate or holographic order of reality is like light, and transcends or generates or unfolds the explicate order of sensory reality. Bohm speculates there may be a super-implicate order which organizes or generates the implicate order as an organizing and active principle. It has the same relationship to the implicate order that consciousness has to matter.

> All of nature is organized according to the activity of significance which, however, can be conceived somatically, in a more subtle form of matter which, in turn, is organized by a still more subtle form of significance. So in that way every level is both somatic and significant. (Ibid., p. 43)

Thus increasing wholes of meaning or significance organize more material parts in an evolution which goes beyond the powers of human thought or imagination. Bohm refrains from identifying any of these orders with God, thus agreeing with our intent. It will be important theological work to draw such distinctions and relationships, not to be attempted here. The point here is that the holographic universe is remarkably congruent with the biblical and mystical witness to the place where humans meet God.

Saint John of the Cross writes of the "luminous darkness" of the experience of God at the culmination of the life of prayer. Meister Eckhart refers to the depth of mystical experience in which the soul in its barrenness, devoid of the scholastic qualities of memory, understanding, and will, meets the Godhead in its entirety. *The Cloud of Unknowing*, as will be described later, goes into precise detail about the arena in which the soul meets God. The description of the holographic or implicate order is stunningly reminiscent of the territory in which the mystics experience the divine presence. The holographic domain seems alike to be the depth of knowing of which humans are capable, the fundamental nature of reality, and the arena for profound prayer.

Does the holoverse express purpose? Whitehead's conception of God, as noted above, is that God is all the potential in the universe and the love drawing us to the fulfillment of that potential. The healing of purpose is the alignment and healing of our limited, partially realized and corrupted purposes in the light of God's loving purpose for us. Does the holographic domain exhibit anything like the loving purpose of the Christian God to "reconcile all things, whether on earth or in heaven?" (Colossians 1:20). It must first be noted that God's purpose has often been misunderstood in a mechanistic Newtonian way. Either a deistic God wound up the machine of the universe in the beginning and did not thereafter interfere with the order he had created, except perhaps for emergency repairs, or God arbitrarily interfered with the natural order to create miracles, perhaps in response to pious prayers. In either case God and universe were assumed to exist as separate subjects and objects in the Newtonian sensory mode. The holoverse is an interconnected whole with the whole enfolded into each of the parts. Purpose would be expressed more in accord with the Buddhist doctrine of Dependent and Simultaneous Origination as a "simultaneous co-operation of all its links insofar as each of them represents the sum total of all the others, seen under a particular aspect," and not necessarily expressed through linear time (Lemko, "Of Holism, Freedom, and the Creative Meaning," p. 82). Such cooperative interdependence of parts and wholes is summarized in the Buddhist saying, "All things arise and pass away."

There is, interestingly enough, some research with animals which suggests a purposive evolution of consciousness even in the animal kingdom. Individual rats, for example, and the whole of a species of rats, seem to be capable of purposive interdependent evolution. W. McDougall at Harvard in 1920, testing the Lamarckian theory of the inheritance of acquired characteristics, began experiments giving carefully bred white rats the task of escaping from a water tank. One gangway out of the tank was brightly lit, but if the rat stepped on it, it received a shock. The second gangway was not illuminated and was safe. There was no shock. In the beginning some of the rats required as many as 330 immersions before they learned decisively to avoid the bright gangway and escape by the safe one. In order to avoid any unconscious selection of quicker learning rats, they were chosen at random before testing and breeding them.

> The experiment was continued for 32 generations and took 15 years to complete. In accordance with the Lamarckian Theory, there was a marked tendency for rats in successive generations to learn more quickly. This is indicated by the average number of errors made by rats in the first eight generations, which was over 56, compared with 41, 29 and 20 in the second, third and fourth groups of eight generations, respectively. The difference was apparent not only in the quantitative results, but also in the actual behavior of the rats, which became more cautious and tentative in the later generations. (Rupert Sheldrake, *A New Science of Life: The Hypothesis of Formative Causation* [Los Angeles: J. P. Tarcher, 1981], p. 187)

McDougall's experimental design and procedures were impeccable and critics were unable to discount them. They did criticize him for not systematically testing change in the rate of learning in rats whose parents had not been trained. Two other groups of experimenters did that. One, W. E. Agar and others at Melbourne, Australia, measured over twenty years the rates of learning of trained and untrained lines for fifty successive generations. "In agreement with McDougall, they found that there was a marked tendency for rats of the trained line to learn more quickly in subsequent generations. *But exactly the same tendency was also found in the untrained line.*" Actually McDougall also observed his untrained lines of rats, although not as systematically, and found the same results. He reported in puzzlement, "It is just possible that the falling off in the average number of errors from 1927 to 1932 represents a real change of constitution of the whole stock, an improvement of it (with respect to this particular faculty) whose nature I am unable to suggest" (ibid., pp. 189-90).

These scientific findings, though impeccable, were disregarded because they were completely inexplicable in light of prevailing biological theories. They suggest that somehow skills in solving the water maze were passed on and "learned" from generation to generation, and *even* to other lines of rats who had not received any training! Somehow information can be directly communicated without the intervention of the senses, and communicated collectively to the species, not just to specific individuals.

Another example of the same phenomenon was observed by scientists studying the Japanese monkey *Macaca fucata*, on the island of Koshima. The scientists provided the monkeys with food by air-dropping sweet potatoes on the beach. In 1952 an eighteen-month-old female named Imo learned to wash the potatoes in a nearby stream before eating them. She taught her mother and playmates to wash their food also. From 1952 to 1958 all the young monkeys on the island and the adults who imitated them came to learn the new behavior. The other adults kept on eating their potatoes in the same old dirty way.

Then in the autumn of 1958 a remarkable event happened. According to the English translation of the Japanese article reporting the research, in a short period of time almost all the rest of the monkeys on the island adopted the new behavior. Even more remarkable, colonies of monkeys on other islands and the mainland troop of monkeys at Takasakiyama began washing their sweet potatoes! Caution should be exercised in accepting these findings, since they reportedly depend on a translation of an ambiguous Japanese phrase regarding the length of time taken for the new behavior to disseminate (Lyall Watson, *Lifetide* [New York: Bantam Books, 1980]).

These observations of monkeys and rats seem hard to swallow. They so contradict our common sense, carefully nurtured on the assumptions of Newtonian physics. But they do make sense in the holographic universe. Perhaps even animals, perhaps animals more naturally than humans, can connect below the sensory level of objects and images into the holographic domain where the common store of information is available to each creature.

The implicate holographic order is displayed as the explicate sensory order. Bohm uses the word *display* as in a readout on a computer screen. We do not see the intimate inner workings of the computer, but we can see some of the results of the working displayed on the screen ("The Physicist and the Mystic—Is a

Dialogue Between Them Possible?" a conversation with David Bohm, conducted by Renee Weber, edited by Emily Selton, *ReVision* 4, no. 1, p. 27). Our sensory experience, and therefore to a large extent our phenomenal experience, is of the displayed explicate order. But we also have more direct access to the implicate order. Worship, prayer, and meditation offer such direct access as will be discussed later. The implicate order also "peeks through" the display or explicate order in events in ordinary life. Carl Jung was puzzled by the appearance of events that could neither be explained as due to cause and effect nor to chance—the possibilities of understanding offered by the Newtonian order. He invented the word *synchronicity* to name "the simultaneous occurrence of a certain psychic state with one or more external events which appear as meaningful parallels to a momentary subjective state—and, in certain cases, vice versa" (C. G. Jung, *Synchronicity*, trans. R. F. Hull [Princeton: Princeton University Press, 1973], p. 25). Persons in analysis with him would dream elaborate visual symbols reproducing the illustrations in an ancient Chinese text he had discovered. Many people recount to their close friends incidents of knowing about a dramatic event before it happens, receiving a direct communication from a loved one at a distance, and indeed, the whole range of what is called paranormal experience. Neither chance nor cause and effect could account for such occurrences. The holoverse, with information about the whole distributed in each part, could, although Jung did not know of that possibility. He simply named the rather common occurrence of another, interdependent dimension of reality peeking through the sensory reality described by classical physics.

What can we make out of all this? Pribram is

known to say at times, "I hope you realize that I don't
*understand* any of this" (Ferguson, "Pribram's
Changing Reality," p. 12). If that is true for Pribram,
it is true many times over for us lay persons
attempting to grasp these frontiers of science. But
they do seem to suggest that our implicit Newtonian
assumptions about prayer may have to be turned on
their heads. For in faithful prayer, we may be literally
in touch with the universe of information far beyond
our sensory capabilities. If that is so, then prayer is
not self-manipulation, but participating in God's
evolving universe. Ken Wilber speculates that this is
the best way to understand human history. For him
"history without Other is history without meaning"
(Ken Wilber, *Up From Eden* [Garden City, N. Y.:
Anchor Press/Doubleday, 1981], p. 3). The panorama
of history is the gradual emergence of humans from
their immersion in nature. At each point in that
emergence, humans grasp and so idolize a partial
conscious wholeness. The attempt to control is
self-defeating, and out of the pain of transition a
greater wholeness is discovered. "Since this wholeness is contiguous with consciousness, itself, we can
also say that *history is the unfolding of human
consciousness*" (ibid., pp. 6-7). History, then, is the
story of humans' collective cooperation with and
resistance to the increasing self-disclosure of the
ultimate reality beneath our individual sensory
experience. God discloses; the human race fears and
welcomes its collective and individual transformation in the light of that disclosure.

# CHAPTER SIX

# Prayer in the Holoverse

Thus far, we have suggested that the implicate order of reality seems very much like the arena in which profound prayer happens as described in biblical and mystical traditions. We have further explored Karl Pribram's theory that the human mind functions holographically and is able to reach below sensory experience to direct contact with the implicate order. Additional current cultural beliefs and clinical research in psychotherapy help describe how prayer connects the mind to the holoverse. These current ideas are again extraordinarily hospitable to biblical and mystical descriptions of prayer and how it operates.

The Pauline tradition in the New Testament particularly suggests that our human vocation is to participate in God's cosmic drama of creation and redemption. We are called to become, each in our own modest way, co-creators with God, not just in our personal lives or only relation to governments and social organizations, or even confined to the physical world itself. We are to cooperate in an immense cosmic drama that we have no adequate way of thinking about or even imagining. Paul writes about it in Romans:

> For the creation waits with eager longing for the revealing of the sons of God; for the creation was subjected to futility, not by its own will, but by the will of him who subjected it in hope; because the creation itself will be set free from its bondage to decay and obtain the glorious liberty of the children of God. We know that the whole creation has been groaning in travail together until now; and not only the creation, but we ourselves, who have the first fruits of the Spirit, groan inwardly, as we wait for our adoption as sons, the redemption of our bodies. For in this hope we were saved. (Romans 8:19-24)

Christ is *logos* or word, God's creative energy who formed all things in the beginning and who will bring them through the drama to their fulfillment under God in the fullness of time. Christ is the Alpha and Omega, the beginning and end of the drama. Christ is the way God created originally according to the Gospel of John and Paul's writing in Colossians: "In the beginning was the Word, and the Word was with God, and the Word was God. He was in the beginning with God; all things are made through him and without him was not anything made. In Christ is all life and the life is the light of human beings. The light shines in the darkness and the darkness does not overcome it" (John 1:1-5).

And finally, Christ is the way God will fulfill the promise of that creation: "God has made known to us in all wisdom and insight the mystery of his will, according to his purpose which he set forth in Christ as a plan for the fulness of time, to unite all things in him, things in heaven and things on earth" (Ephesians 1:9, 10).

We do not know, of course, what the consummation will look like. The revelation is of the brightness of the promise, not its game plan. New Testament writers strain their metaphoric resources to give hints of the intuition:

> Then I saw a new heaven and a new earth; for the first heaven and the first earth had passed away, and the sea was no more. And I saw the holy city, new Jerusalem, coming down out of heaven from God, prepared as a bride adorned for her husband; and I heard a loud voice from the throne saying, "Behold, the dwelling of God is with men. He will dwell with them, and they shall be his people, and God himself will be with them; He will wipe away every tear from their eyes, and death shall be no more, neither shall there be mourning nor crying nor pain any more, for the former things have passed away." (Revelation 21:1-4)

In between the Alpha and the Omega, the metaphoric beginning and end (since even time itself is subject to transformation), is the drama. In the struggle there is all the glory and suffering of human and natural history. Christ, the creating and redeeming Word, is of course essential to the completion of that drama. Incredible as it may sound, each one of us is also essential.

Prayer is the general name for the ways in which we intend to fulfill that awesome commission of co-creatorship. Paul in Romans immediately after the description of the cosmic drama quoted above explains how we are to participate in it: "Likewise the Spirit helps us in our weakness; for we do not know how to pray as we ought, but the Spirit himself intercedes for us with sighs too deep for words. And he who searches the hearts of men knows what is the mind of the Spirit, because the Spirit intercedes for the saints according to the will of God" (Romans 8:26-27).

We can suggest, using the ideas of the previous chapter, that God's cosmic drama is played out in the interconnected holistic reality of the holoverse and displayed sensorially in time and space. To cooperate in that drama as co-creators, we must then reach below our sensory experience to the holistic information available in the holoverse. Pribram demonstrates that the brain-mind system is constructed holographically and is able to do precisely that. Prayer in the Christian tradition is the way we intend to reach directly to the implicate order that we may cooperate with God's purpose in the unique way each of us is called to do.

Prayer, then, is alignment, the "lining up" or guiding of our phenomenal experience and actions with the holistic information available to us in the holoverse. The traditional Christian term for this alignment is *discernment*. The word comes from the Greek *diakrisis*, "cutting through." It is sometimes misleadingly transliterated "discretion." But it is not being discrete, except in a very special sense. It is cutting through the confusion and limitations of our sensory experience to the clear light of God's wisdom made available to us in the holographic domain of our mind.

And here we come to a critical distinction. Fritjof Capra parallels physical and mystical methods of investigation of reality.

Physicists explore levels of matter, mystics explore levels of mind . . . on the one hand you have scientists probing into matter with the help of very sophisticated instruments, and, on the other hand, you have mystics probing into consciousness with very sophisticated techniques of meditation. Both reach non-ordinary levels of perception, and at these non-ordinary levels, it seems that the patterns, and principles of organization that they observe are very similar. ("The Tao of Physics Revisited," a conversation with Fritjof Capra conducted by Renee Weber, *ReVision* 4, no. 1, p. 44)

The conclusions are similar, but the methods, although equally rigorous, are very different. For example, the scientist, as Capra notes, uses sophisticated instruments. The mystic has no such intermediaries to sharpen perception but goes unaided to the depths of unique personal experience. The scientist with proper qualifications can generalize findings to other situations and even general laws. The mystic, if precise, can only testify to her own experience and invite others to their quest. The scientist can build on the cumulative work of others, not needing to repeat earlier experiments, but using their findings as a basis for later work. The mystic does not have it so easy. One can study the sacred texts and the teachings of others, but they mean nothing until they are discovered in the joy and pain and discipline of one's own prayer life. Every mystic has to start from scratch, living his or her own unique life of prayer from the beginning, regardless of what exalted states others may have reached.

But the essential difference is one of purpose. The scientist wishes to understand. The Christian mystic wishes to love. The scientist searches for general patterns by which to explain and predict the occurrences of events; the mystic wishes to manifest the love of God in all the events of a singular human life. The scientist strives to eliminate subjective bias, inaccurate data gathering, and incorrect reasoning. The mystic attempts to eliminate egocentricity, to fulfill the law of love. Modern physicists and brain-mind researchers reach the holographic domain beneath the display of sensory experience. Mystics seek to reach and manifest the universal love of God beneath distracted and egocentric thoughts, feelings, and behaviors.

The scientist, if well funded, has marvelous technological devices like cyclotrons and biofeedback machines as resources in the search for understanding. The Christian mystic has only the instructions of our Lord: "You shall love the Lord your God with all your heart, and with all your soul, and with all your mind. This is the great and first commandment. And a second is like it, You shall love your neighbor as yourself" (Matthew 22:37-39).

It seems incredible that, given such different methods, scientists and mystics should reach such congruent understandings of reality. Scientists have found an interconnected holoverse displayed in sensory experience. Mystics find the universal love of God working out the cosmic drama of redemption through personal lives and world history. Scientists do not seek to abolish or discount sensory experience, but to understand it in the larger context of the holoverse. Wise mystics do not try to abolish or discount their individual, unique human lives and personalities, but to align and transform them in God's loving purpose. (It is possible to draw some connections between the lenslike character of sensory experience and egocentricity. The lens, as noted earlier, by focusing tends to objectify, separating subject from object. Egocentricity also separates subject from object, and self from others. Both sensory experience and individual or self-centered experience are derivative or secondary realities.)

Discernment is the process of aligning human and divine purpose. It is the aim and the nature of prayer. Discernment was described as the healing of purpose in the first chapter. Our partially realized and contaminated purposes are healed, aligned, and fulfilled as God's purposes for us in discernment. Decision actualizes the healing of purpose. In deciding to receive God's name—in deciding to act in ministry—purpose and behavior are linked and realized. We decide in order to realize some purpose. There is no decision without purpose, only random activity. We decide by doing something, by engaging in concrete behavior. Without behavior, there is no decision, only speculation and discussion.

The decision of discernment links God's saving initiative and our human response. There is no decision in faith unless it is God's gracious initiative toward us. Against Calvin, there is no faith decision unless we decide to own God's initiative. Decision implies relationship. God and we must conspire in this. We become truly ourselves; our purpose is healed as God becomes truly God for us. By grace we intend what God intends. That is the moment of salvation and the moment of ministry as well.

The decision of discernment also links the theology and the practice of ministry. The gap between academic and practical theology is the absence of decision. Theologians justify or rationalize decisions. Ministers learn functional skills and practice them. Decision is the act of faith that unites our faith convictions and our doing of ministry.

Prayer is realized in decision. In the liturgy, in pastoral action, in the common prayer of the church, and in our personal prayer, we receive God's name for us and act to realize it. Decision links our human perception and action in sensory experience with the holistic information of God's loving purpose in the holoverse. Thus both in terms of Christian prayer and modern scientific understanding of reality, the decision of discernment makes manifest or displays the hidden fundamental reality in human action in time and space.

As the least lenslike of the senses, touch seems the proper sensory metaphor for praying, as seeing was for Augustine's loving, and hearing for Calvin's knowledge. Touch is the most intimate of senses. We must be very close to people in order to touch them. Touching is a personal act; we decide and own our relationship with others when we touch them. If someone touches us impersonally or objectively, we feel violated. And if someone touches us violently, we are personally hurt beyond the capabilities of speaking or looking.

Touch is the most modest of senses. There is no pretension to grasping the nature of the whole as one can do in seeing. The parable of the six blind men touching an elephant has made that point for centuries. Yet in its modesty touch penetrates to essence. When I touch you, I am in touch with you, not only with some peripheral aspect. The touch in love melts the heart, gets to me, goes beneath the surface. Finally, touch is essentially action. I can see and hear without participating, but I must act in order to touch.

Prayer, then, is discernment, actualizing the healing of purpose in decision, as both modern science and the biblical and mystical tradition suggest. In the prayer of discernment, human beings are transformed to realize their co-creatorship with God in the cosmic drama of creation and redemption. The healing of purpose is itself this transformation of all levels of personhood that we may indeed become a new creation.

# CHAPTER SEVEN

# Prayer and the Will

The last two chapters described a contemporary understanding of the holoverse as the arena for profound prayer. Prayer makes sense in that reality as it has not since the rise of classical physics. Changing cultural beliefs have also transformed our self-understanding. Augustine rightly put the issue as one of will. Discernment is a process of transforming the will to love God. However, the strategies for transforming the will used in Christian history were often harsh applications of current cultural prejudices about the will and how to subdue it. Conscious, even obsessive self-monitoring and self-manipulation of the emotions were often taught as ways of controlling the will. Prayer that depends on such harsh and even violent methods is no longer credible. Modern social science has radically revised our understanding of the will and how it operates. Specifically, we know more about the influence of social determinates on willing, psychophysiological maturing of the will, the role of the unconscious and parts of the psyche, and the embodiment of the will. This chapter will describe how these new developments lay a more adequate foundation for understanding how prayer happens.

Our knowledge of the will has dramatically increased in the last hundred years, most significantly since Sigmund Freud inaugurated the cultural revolution called depth psychology with the publication of *Studies in Hysteria* in 1896. The explosion of empirical interest in the human psyche from then until today has been immense. For Augustine the critical issue had to do with willing to love God instead of the phenomenal world. If the purpose of prayer is to manifest God's love, then understanding how human beings love and will to love is critical to understanding how prayer operates. The following developments have changed and increased that understanding.

First, our interest in the human mind has shifted from a normative to a more descriptive interest. The finely drawn anecdotal portraits of the vicissitudes of will in some Christian pastoral literature had a normative aim. The concern of Christian pastors was to mold the human will to the will of God, and whatever empirical interest there was in the will as it actually operated was only for that purpose. Freud celebrated the empirical interest in the human will for its own sake. He was fascinated with how the human mind actually operated, not by how it was supposed to operate.

Because of that empirical interest, our understanding of loving and willing has dramatically increased.

Of all that we know now about ourselves that we did not know about ourselves a century ago, perhaps three findings are particularly significant for willing. The first is that our wills are determined more by the social organizations to which we belong and the roles we play in them than they are by our personal preferences. Durkheim demonstrated that suicide, that extreme form of willing against oneself, was statistically significantly different between Catholics and Protestants, and between single people and married people. In the Christian tradition we have addressed the human will all these centuries as if it existed all by itself in isolation from its social and physical environment. Now we have learned to take those environmental factors into account as necessary and important weights or factors in our willing.

The second effect of empirical interest in the human psyche is to discover that we have a childhood. As Philippe Aries in *Centuries of Childhood: A Social History of Family Life* (New York: Random House, 1965) pointed out, childhood is a recent development in European civilization. For most of Christian history children were regarded as little adults. And their wills were to be trained and controlled by the same strategies used with adults. A vivid example is given by Susanna Wesley, who at her son John's request, described her own (to him, exemplary) Christian child-reading practices. It is quoted at some length here because it details the painstaking ways reflective self-consciousness is awakened and the will subdued as early as possible. Richard Heitzenrater has recently broken the codes in which John Wesley recorded and evaluated his own spiritual progress in his diary over a lifetime. Wesley kept a description of his activities for each hour of the day, evaluating each activity during the hour on a six-point scale of fervor. For example, at Morning Prayer, his response to each collect, scripture reading, and other portions of the service was recorded and evaluated separately. Then the hour itself was evaluated according to "Temper of Devotion" and a second scale. Then a miscellaneous set of evaluative codes was added for the hour for such matters as "temptation escaped," and "blessing received." Finally, the whole day was summarized and evaluated. This understanding of the life of prayer as continuous compulsive self-monitoring and conscious self-evaluation seems to follow naturally from his mother's convictions about the human will as expressed in her child-rearing practices.

> When turned a year old (and some before), they were taught to fear the rod and to cry softly; by which means they escaped abundance of correction they might otherwise have had, and that most odious noise of the crying of children was rarely heard in the house, but the family usually lived in as much quietness as if there had not been a child among them.
>
> As soon as they were grown pretty strong, they were confined to three meals a day. At dinner their little table and chairs were set by ours, where they could be overlooked; and they were suffered to eat and drink (small beer) as much as they would; but not to call for anything. If they wanted aught they used to whisper to the maid which attended them, who came and spake to me; and as soon as they could handle a knife and fork, they were never suffered to choose their meat, but always made eat such things as were provided for the family.
>
> . . . But whatever they had, they were never permitted to eat at those meals of more than one thing, and of that sparingly enough. . . . Nor were they suffered to go into the kitchen to ask anything of the servants when they are at meat; if it was known they did, they were certainly beat and the servants severely reprimanded.

At six, as soon as family prayers were over, they had their supper; at seven the maid washed them, and, beginning at the youngest, she undressed and got them all to bed by eight; at which time she left them in the several rooms awake—for there was no such thing allowed of in our house as sitting by a child till it fell asleep.

They were so constantly used to eat and drink what was given them that, when any of them was ill, there was no difficulty in making them take the most unpleasant medicine; for they durst not refuse it, though some of them would presently throw it up. . . .

In order to form the minds of children, the first thing to be done is to conquer their will and bring them to an obedient temper. To inform the understanding is a work of time and must with children proceed by slow degrees as they are able to bear it; but the subjection of the will is a thing that must be done at once, and the sooner the better. For by neglecting timely correction, they will contract a stubbornness and obstinacy which is hardly ever after conquered; and never, without using such severity as would be as painful to me as to the child. . . . Whenever a child is corrected, it must be conquered; and this will be no hard matter to do if it be not grown headstrong by too much indulgence. And when the will of a child is totally subdued, and it is brought to revere and stand in awe of its parents, then a great many childish follies and inadvertencies may be passed by. . . . I insist upon conquering the will of children betimes, because this is the only strong and rational foundation of a religious education, without which both precept and example will be ineffective. . . .

I cannot yet dismiss the subject. As self-will is the root of all sin and misery, so whatever cherishes this in children ensures their after-wretchedness and irreligion; whatever checks and mortifies it promotes their future happiness and piety. This is still more evident if we further consider that religion is nothing else than the doing the will of God, and not our own; that, the one grand impediment to our temporal and eternal happiness being this self-will, no indulgences of it can be trivial, no denial unprofitable. Heaven or hell depends on this alone. So that the parent who studies to subdue it in his child works together with God in the renewing and saving of souls. . . .

They were quickly made to understand they might have nothing they cried for, and instructed to speak handsomely for what they wanted. They were not suffered to ask even the lowest servant for aught without saying, 'Pray give me such a thing'; and the servant was chid if she ever let them omit that word. Taking God's name in vain, cursing and swearing, profanities, obscenity, crude, ill-bred names, were never heard among them. Nor were they ever permitted to call each other by their proper names without the addition of Brother or Sister. . . .

One day was allowed the child whenever to learn its letters, and each of them did in that time know all its letters, great and small, except Molly and Nancy, who were a day and a half before they knew them perfectly; for which I then thought them very dull, but since I have observed how long many children are learning the horn-book, I have changed my opinion. . . .

There was no such thing as loud talking or playing allowed of but that everyone was kept close to their business, for the six hours of school. . . .

Rising out of their places, or going out of the room, was not permitted unless for good cause; and running into the yard, garden, or street without leave was always esteemed a capital offence. (Nehemiah Curnock, ed., *The Journal of John Wesley* [London: The Epworth Press, 1960] 3:34-39)

Now we have discovered that human beings go through stages. The will of the small child does not operate like the will of the adult. Erik Erikson gave us one map of the life stages through which we must go. Lawrence Kohlberg and Carol Gilligan have described the moral reasoning possible and appropriate at different stages. Hundreds of researchers have described in exhaustive detail what it is like to be middle-aged or elderly. Each stage of life—not just childhood—has its own characteristic challenges to successful coping and thriving, or exercise of the will. As a result, we can become more compassionate and gentle with ourselves, not expecting of a two-year-old what we expect of a twenty-year-old. We can reject forcible and even violent attempts to train the will by premature and even obsessive self-consciousness and self-monitoring.

We have also discovered that the will is embodied. One of the tragic ironies of the Christian faith is that we emphasize a theological doctrine of embodiment symbolically and dogmatically and ignore it in our religious practice to a degree almost unknown among the world's great religions. From Hindu yoga to Sufi dancing, saints and mystics have known that the body is a powerful means for the transformation of the will. But the believers in the Incarnation, the Word made flesh, have been singularly ignorant about the flesh in religious pratice. There are sporadic exceptions from the Desert Fathers to the Shakers. But by and large it remained to modern psychologists and increasing dialogue with other religions to remind us of what this central tenet of our faith might actually mean. Because of their pioneering efforts, we are now beginning to understand how breathing, posture, muscular tone, relaxation, and grace of movement are powerful aids to expressions of a loving will.

But perhaps the most significant legacy of modern psychology for the will is this: we have discovered that we have parts. The statement is absurdly simple. Paul well knew it,

> For I delight in the law of God, in my inmost self, but I see in my members another law at war with the law of my mind and making me captive to the law of sin which

dwells in my members. Wretched man that I am! Who
will deliver me from this body of death? Thanks be to
God through Jesus Christ our Lord! So then, I of myself
serve the law of God with my mind, but with my flesh I
serve the law of sin. (Romans 7:22-25)

But though he knew it, it remained to modern
psychology to sort out and explore the parts of the
psyche that interact in subtle and complex ways in
willing to love. These parts of the psyche are
extraordinarily hard to pin down. They are evidently
not like tables and chairs in the external world that
can be identified and counted once and for all
because they are what they seem and they stay what
they are. The parts of the psyche seem to shift and
transmute. Different psychologists call them by
different names. And the different names do not even
seem to be alternate designations of the same
entities, but refer to different dimensions of the
psyche altogether.

Some schools of psychology have tried to be as
simple about it as possible, identifying certain
learning patterns we share at least with rats, and
ignoring the "black box" of the inner experience of
the psyche. Carl Jung tried to be as comprehensive
about it as possible, introducing dimensions of the
psyche usually considered explicitly religious. But
whether they are subpersonalities (psychosynthesis);
ego states (transactional analysis); shadow, anima,
archetype, and self (Jung); id, ego, and superego
(Freud); or something else, it seems to be agreed: we
have parts.

What, then, is a part of the psyche? At the risk of
seeming dilettante in dealing with so much careful
theorizing, it nevertheless seems clear: a part of the
psyche is a center of purpose. It is an aspect of the

psyche that intends something for the sake of the organism and wills through certain behaviors to achieve it. The nurturing parent ego state in TA wills to nurture and comfort myself or others. "Uncle George" or the "Sherriff" as I call one of my subpersonalities in a psychosynthesis mode, wills to have adventures in my life as Uncle George did (or at least as I perceived and internalized him). My anima is my soul, the other-sexed bridge that wills to relate my conscious ego to the rest of my psyche and especially to the emerging self.

It is in Freud's categories that the notion that a part is a center of purpose seems especially clear. Bruno Bettelheim has criticized Lynn Strachey and the "official" translations of Freud's writing into English for intentional mistranslations of key terms (Bruno Bettelheim, *Freud and Man's Soul* [New York: Alfred A. Knopf, 1982]).

Strachey's translation, Bettelheim speculates, was especially influenced by American psychoanalysts. American psychoanalysts were all physicians, determined to keep psychoanalysis a medical specialty despite Freud's own expressed opposition to that direction. To do so, they wanted Freud to sound as medical and as scientific in English as possible. They saw his work as *Naturwissenschaften*, or natural science, even though Freud came to regard his own work more in the realm of *Geisteswissenschaften*, or humanities.

Since Freud didn't think much of Americans anyway, he did not protest the American editions. But the mistranslations of three key terms are especially important for understanding a part of the psyche as a center of purpose. *Id*, *ego*, and *superego* do not exist in the German. They are made-up words of Greek derivation to suggest, presumably, their

medical-scientific-esoteric precision. Freud had something quite different in mind. The words he used are
*Ich, Uberich,* and *es: I, over-I,* and *it* respectively. By
"I," he meant just what he wrote, the personal willing
center of identity and purpose. The "over-I" referred to
the I-ness one internalizes from parents and other
authority figures. The "it" is most interesting. "It" is
the pronoun adults use to refer to children. "It" is the
unsocialized, spontaneous I-ness of children.

All three are centers of purpose. The center of
purpose I call "I" has the delicate task of integrating
and balancing the other centers of purpose. Particularly "I" need to integrate the unsocialized I-ness of
childhood in my functioning as an adult. For Freud, it
was reclamation work.

The unassuming term *part* comes from neuro-lin-
guistic programming, developed by Richard Bandler
and John Grinder. Their theories and methods
developed from careful observation and coding of the
formal patterns effective psychotherapists use, regardless of the theories by which the therapists
themselves describe their work. The person from
whom they learned most was Milton Erikson, whom
some regard as the most important psychotherapist
in recent history. Erickson primarily used what are
called hypnotic methods, which intend direct communication with the unconscious.

Bandler and Grinder, like Erickson, and like Freud
before them, have concluded that most human
behavior is unconscious. Our thoughts, our feelings,
images and body sensations, even our bodily move-
ments and our interactions with other people exist
for the most part outside of our conscious awareness.
Most of the time, we do not know what we are
thinking, feeling, and doing. In fact, as Freud
discovered, even many of our conscious thoughts

about what we are doing are rationalizations, after-the-fact justifications which have little to do with what we actually did and why.

The parts of our psyche, then, are often partly or mostly unconscious. We find ourselves doing something and often do not know that we did it or why. But this is not counsel to despair. It is to dramatically reorient our understanding of willing to love. If we want to love as Jesus commanded, it is not enough to give ourselves conscious moral exhortations or to receive them from others. We need to dialogue with our unconscious. Specifically we need to dialogue with the part or center of purpose in ourselves that is willing some behavior we wish either to commend or to change.

The "I," the fragile, integrating center of purpose, has the task of managing the partial centers of purpose within that together make up the totality of my willing to love. To do so, I must dialogue with the unconscious and partially unconscious parts that contribute to that totality. There are three assumptions necessary for that dialogue.

The first is to distinguish between purpose and behavior. The behavior that part expresses, e. g., withdrawing from contact with people in new situations, is not the same as its purpose. In fact we often cannot even deduce the purpose from the behavior. That particular behavior may have made sense in a very different context as an effective expression of the purpose of the part. But today in this context it is totally mystifying. If I want to change the behavior, I must learn the usually unconscious purpose behind it.

The second assumption is that the purpose behind the behavior is beneficent, it intends my good. No matter how bizarre or detrimental that behavior now seems, its original purpose was in some way to enhance my survival and well-being. This assumption seems to clash with Augustine's distrust of his human loves, and certainly with Calvin's conviction of the total depravity of the will. It raises a fundamental theological question. But it makes sense in the holographic universe. As Kenneth Wilber wrote, every partial purpose is a premature human attempt to grasp wholeness. By grasping and attempting to control it for our own sake, our partial wholeness becomes an idolatry.

In prayer by God's grace we can trace and heal that partial purpose back into God's whole and complete purpose for our life and situation. In God's redeeming love we can intend more closely what God intends, being reunited to the ground of our partial purpose in the ultimate reality of God's love. That at least is a faith conviction. Those who hold that our purposes are evil, not partial, will have to find some other inexplicable way to pray and to love God and neighbor.

Most human behavior is a communication. We mean something by what we do, and our behavior is our way of communicating that meaning. The third assumption is that if we wish to change behavior, we need to change its meaning or purpose or context. Bandler and Grinder call changing the context "reframing," and it is their basic therapeutic strategy. Reframing is "changing the frame in which a person perceives events in order to change the meaning. When the meaning changes, the person's responses and behavior also change" (Richard Bandler and John Grinder, *Reframing* [Moab, Utah: Real People Press, 1982], p. 1).

These contemporary ideas about the human psyche enable us to better understand how the healing of

purpose happens in the prayer of discernment.
Healing of purpose is a reframing, a setting of the
behavior prayed about in the larger purpose of God's
loving purpose for the one who prays. That larger
purpose is disclosed as the prayer reaches below
conscious sensory experience to the guiding presence
of God in the implicate order of the holoverse. That
presence transforms or heals the purpose of the one
who prays, and thus reframes or changes the
resulting behavior. Reframing, then, happens
through the artful dialogue between conscious
sensory experience and the unconscious depths. The
conscious mind has a necessary but very limited role
in that process. Michael Polanyi's distinction between subsidiary and focal awareness helps us
understand the role of consciousness in that dialogue.
When we are learning to play a new piece on the
piano, for example, we pay explicit attention to the
various parts of the whole experience. We read the
notes, work out the fingering, decide on tempo, and so
on. That is subsidiary awareness. When we have
learned the piece and perform it, we no longer pay
attention to the fingering as such. We experience our
performing as a whole in focal awareness. In fact, if
we suddenly relapse to the subsidiary awareness of
our fingering, the performance falters or stops. We
can only play the music beautifully in focal awareness, paying attention to the whole experience and
trusting the various parts to be handled outside of
conscious awareness. Subsidiary awareness is functional when learning a new skill. When it is learned, it
"streamlines," as Bandler and Grinder say, slipping
into the unconscious so that our conscious mind can
focally attend to the whole experience. Graceful and
skillful action depends upon trusting the unconscious
to attend to the myriad details involved in even

simple behavior, so that the conscious mind can
enjoy and enhance the totality of the experience
through focal awareness. It is the curse of the
neurotic not to trust the process, anxiously monitor-
ing and analyzing the parts of any experience, unable
to be present to or enjoy the experience itself. In
doing so, the activity is often clumsily carried out
because the conscious mind was unable to do its
proper task of focal awareness.

Prayer can be thought of as reframing, involving
dialogue between conscious and unconscious states
of mind. The conscious mind can handle only small
amounts of data at a time. Research indicates that
only seven bits of information, plus or minus two in
varying cases, can be consciously and simultaneously
attended to. Since even walking involves handling
many times that complexity of information, it is clear
that the proper role of the conscious mind is severely
restricted to such matters as planning, evaluating,
learning or correcting specific behaviors, dialoging
with the unconscious, and attending to the flow of
experience. In prayer as reframing, our conscious
mind articulates or names the purposes we discern
and the decisions by which we actualize them in
behavior. That is a theological task. What God
reveals to us in the prayer of discernment is a
consciously recognized name—a name for our condition and what we are to do about it. It sometimes is
not easily recognizable. Often it is a subtle intuition
we must discern with patience. Nevertheless it is a
dramatic naming, a cutting through of the confusion
of our life to some clarity. The naming is a fundamental, conscious understanding about the nature of
reality; and in this sense it is accurate to call it
theological insight. Theology refers to the ways we
understand God, ourselves, and the world. Theology

is a decision because it is a way of naming reality; more specifically, it is the place the scripture and tradition and our personal experience intersect. Theological insight in this context can be described the way G. Spencer Brown describes mathematics. It consists of insights or ways "powerful in comparison with others, of revealing our internal knowledge of the structure of the world" (G. Spencer Brown, *Laws of Form* [New York: Julian Press, 1972], p. xvii).

Our theological naming in prayer is the intuitive recognition that this is the way the world really is, and we knew it all the time, but we didn't know that we knew it. Brown, comparing mathematics to psychoanalysis, writes a sentence that could also be applied to theological insight: "In each discipline, we attempt to find out, by a mixture of contemplation, symbolic representation, communion and communication, what it is we already know" (ibid., p. xix). Theological insight, in this view, is the expansion of our awareness into consciousness. Like "a recognizable aspect of mathematics" in Brown's view, it "consists in the advancement of the consciousness of what we are doing, whereby the covert becomes overt. Mathematics is in this respect psychedelic" (ibid., p. 85).*

Theological naming is not simply a matter of making linguistic distinctions. It is a way of giving internal instructions to the rest of the nervous system

---

*One implication of this view is the intuitive and problematic relation of theological insight to ordinary language. Our common speech is a treasure store of our common human experience. When theology becomes too abstracted from human experience, it may lose its source and its credibility. Again, Brown's words about mathematics can be applied also to theological insight: "There seems to be no mathematical [theological] idea of any importance or profundity that is not mirrored, with an almost uncanny accuracy, in the common use of words. And this appears especially true when we consider words in their original, and sometimes long forgotten, senses."

to occasion psychophysiological transformation, as we shall see later. John Lilly suggests that "the cerebral cortex functions as a high-level computer controlling the structurally lower levels of the nervous system. It is a biocomputer. When one uses language or symbols, analyzes, makes metaphors, or, in short *learns to learn*, one is 'metaprogramming' the human biocomputer" (in Michael Talbot, *Mysticism and the New Physics* [New York: Bantam Books, 1981], p. 149). Metaprograms are what we really believe, the fundamental values and world views by which we live our lives; and they have profound effects upon us. Metaprograms based upon the Newtonian order can even make us sick. Larry Dossey, a physician, lists "increased gastric acid secretion; increased blood cholesterol; an increased respiratory rate; increased secretory activity of sweat glands; and increased muscle tension throughout the body" as a result of what he calls "hurry sickness" or the "time syndrome" (Dossey, *Time, Space and Medicine*, pp. 50, 51). This syndrome is the fervent belief in the fundamental reality of linear time—that time proceeds irrevocably in linear fashion as the clocks we have created and Newtonian physics tell us it does. Accompanying this belief is an inward sense of urgency by which individuals metaprogram and drive their psychophysiology to stress, to the medical symptoms listed above, and sometimes to heart attacks and physical death.

Prayer as dialogue between conscious mind and unconscious depths not only changes our behavior and even our body, but it also restructures the eternal reality we then experience. Jesus' teachings on faith have been an embarrassment to liberal theologians for centuries, with their clear implication that we can even restructure material reality. "Even if you say to this mountain, 'Get up and throw youself into sea,' it will be done. And if you have faith, everything you ask for in prayer you will receive" (Matthew 21:21-22 JB). But if the implicate order of the holoverse is the realm of infinite possibilities, and the mind can actualize and display them in sensory experience, those teachings make very good sense. Again modern physics can help us understand how our faith expressed in our perceptions actually creates reality.

One of the best illustrations involves the controversy over whether light is fundamentally like a wave or like a particle. In 1803 Thomas Young settled the matter once and for all, he was sure, in a simple and dramatic experiment. He set up a light source and put in front of it a screen with two vertical slits. In front of that was a wall (Zukav, *The Dancing Wu Li Masters*, p. 60).

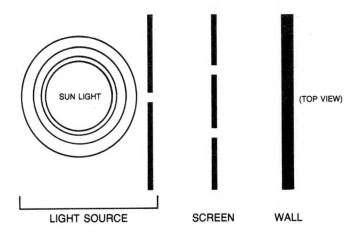

When one slit is covered, and the light comes through the other, the wall is illuminated, as shown in the diagram on page 130, by a circle of light.

When both slits are uncovered, however, an amazing thing happens. The projection on the wall should be the sum of the light from the two slits, but it is not. Instead the wall is illuminated with alternating bands of light and darkness.

The alternating light and dark bands are a well-known phenomenon of wave mechanics called interference. Interference results when the waves of light diffracting from the two slits interfere with each other. In some places the waves overlap and reinforce one another. In other places they cancel each other. Young's experiment demonstrated that light must be wave-like because only waves can create interference patterns.

However, Einstein, working from Phillipe Lenard's experimental work, demonstrated that light must be particle-like. Lenard showed that the flow of electrons in the photoelectric effect begins immediately when the impinging light strikes the target metal. According to the wave theory of light, the electrons in a metal should only start to jiggle when struck by light waves, and not come out of it until they are moving fast enough. If they come out immediately, they must be particles, not waves (ibid., pp. 53-54).

So now we have a remarkable state of affairs. Since Einstein demonstrated that light is composed of particles called photons, what happens when a single photon goes through Young's experiment? If the second slit is closed, it may go through the first slit and land on an area of the wall *that would be dark if the second slit were open.* The question is, then, how did the photon know that the second slit was not open? If both slits are open, there are always alternating bands of light and dark. That means there are always areas where photons never go (hence the dark areas). If one of the slits is closed, there is no interference and the dark bands disappear. The whole wall becomes illuminated, including the areas that were dark when both slits are open. How does the photon "know" that it can go to an area that must be dark if the other slit were open, i. e., how does the photon "know" that the other slit is closed? (ibid., p. 63).

Such questions plunge us into the unthinkable, according to conventional reality. Are photons capable of receiving information from a distance and making conscious decisions in relation to it? Quantum mechanics, the theoretical foundation of much of modern physics, approaches such questions by giving up the attempt to predict what will actually happen in favor of the more modest, but realizable goal of predicting the probability of various alternative results. Rather than trying to predict where the single photon will land when it goes through the slot (and dealing with the conundrum of how it knows whether or not the other slit is open), physicists describe several possible results and the probabilities of their happening. Schrodinger's wave equation governs the description of a whole range of possibilities which just keep on unfolding until one of them actualizes (ibid., pp. 65-66). These ranges of possibilities are called probability waves. They are mathematical entities which predict the probability of certain events occurring or not occurring. They refer to what somehow already is happening, but has not been actualized. They refer to a tendency to happen that in some undefined way exists of itself, even if it never becomes an event. Heisenberg wrote:

> It meant a tendency for something. It was a quantitative version of the old concept of "potentia" in Aristotelian philosophy. It introduced something standing in the middle between the idea of an event and the actual event, a strange kind of physical reality, just in the middle or between possibility and reality. (Ibid., p. 66)

How do we find out what is really happening? Physicists carefully isolate a "region of preparation" (the light source, the slits, the wall) and a "region of measurement" (a photographic plate) from the seamless web of the universe. In this artificial, idealized, and isolated area they correlate what happens between the observables (mathematical statements of), the production and detection of the light. The correlation is a concept, a statement of relationships between the observables. The photon observed is not like a table or chair; it is not a thing, but a relationship. It does not exist by itself. It is not material reality as we understand that in conventional thought. It is a relationship which is realized in the interaction of the production and detection of light.

What causes the relationship to become actual? If the various possibilities continue to unfold according to the probability waves, what causes this relationship to be realized, to become an actual event in this world? What causes a possibility to become an actuality? The answer: our measuring it. Making a measurement interferes with the development of possibilities. In doing so we actualize one of several potentialities and nullify the others. Suppose one photon detector is placed at slit one, and another photon detector is placed at slit two. A photon is emitted from the light source. There are two possibilities for it. It can go through slit one or it can go through slit two. Each of these possibilities is included in the wave function of that photon.

When we examine the detectors we find that number two has fired. As soon as we know this, we know that the photon did not go through slit one, and therefore, that possibility no longer exists. Therefore the wave function of the photon has changed. Physicists call this the collapse of the wave function. It is the abrupt collapse of all the developing aspects of the wave function except the one that actualizes (ibid.).

The wave function collapses when the measurement is made. That is the intervention which actualizes one event and eliminates the potential of other events happening, in this world at least. Therefore it is our *looking* which actualizes, creates the event in this sense. The trouble with accepting this idea is our commonsense view, held with the authority of Newtonian physics, that objects are either there or they are not, regardless of whether or not we perceive them. That simply is not the case in quantum mechanics. To make the point, there is the metaphor of Schrodinger's cat. The cat is locked in a box, and a randomly activated lever either does or does not release a poison gas which can kill the cat instantly. There is no way of knowing, short of opening the box, whether the gas has been released and the cat is dead. Common sense and classical physics tell us the cat is either dead or alive, and all we have to do is open the box to find out. But in quantum mechanics our perception actualizes the events of the cat's fate. There are different ways of interpreting what happens. According to the historic Copenhagen conference in 1927, "the cat is in a kind of limbo represented by a wave function which contains the possibility that the cat is dead and also the possibility that the cat is alive. When we look in the box, and not before, one of these possibilities actualizes and the other vanishes" (ibid., p. 85-86).

Another theory proposed by some physicists claims that the wave function is real. Therefore, all of the possibilities it represents are real and they all happen. Appropriately, it is called the Many Worlds Interpretation, because it suggests that all of the possibilities are actualized simultaneously in alternate universes. Therefore, if Schrodinger's cat is discovered alive here, it is dead in another world.

Our perception creates the visible universe by selecting some potential possibility and actualizing it. That statement is startling enough. What is even more astounding is to entertain the question, "Who is looking?" Suppose a machine automatically triggers when a photon passes. At that point the measurement collapses and actualizes the event. Suppose a technician is watching the machine trigger, and his perception of the machine's perception actualizes the event. Suppose the physicist who is head of the laboratory watches the technician running the equipment, and his perception of the technician's perception of the machine's perception actualizes the event. Suppose God . . . And so this abstruse discussion of modern physics leads directly back to the mystic experience in which full awareness creates in the act of experiencing things arising and passing away—the way things really are. But it is not the mystic as a separated, isolated self who thus creates in the act of experiencing. For the mystic is preoccupied with the question, "Who is looking?" Who is actualizing the universe in every moment? As Talbot suggests, "The universe embraces all possibilities because the consciousness can conceive all possibilities" (Talbot, *Mysticism and the New Physics*, p. 139). The holoverse frees us from metaprogrammed entrapment in sensory reality as the only reality there is. Jesus leads us to understand the infinite possibilities of God's love which can restructure even physical reality. Faith is the prayer of discernment that reframes egocentric purpose into larger purposes of God's love, actualizes new possibilities of loving behavior, and literally changes the world.

Prayer of discernment of this significance involves a discipline and commitment far beyond the usual Christian understanding of prayer. Perhaps because we have given up the expectation that prayer can change anything in the Newtonian order, we have given up on prayer itself. We don't expect much from prayer, and we don't practice it much or deeply. In the next chapters we shall suggest something of what the practice of prayer might be like. The prayer of discernment as reframing changes the metaprograms, thereby changing our perception and so altering or restructing reality. It does so specifically by directly affecting the central nervous system and through it the psychophysiology of the whole human organism. The description of time sickness above demonstrates that the metaprogram through the nervous system literally changes tissue. The fact is now commonplace in medical research, however physicians may wish to hide from its implications by calling it the "placebo effect." An impeccable scientific study on the chances for survival from atherosclerotic heart disease found that "the most reliable factor in determining survival was not smoking, high blood pressure, diabetes mellitus, or high blood cholesterol levels, but *job satisfaction*. And the second best predictor was what the task force termed 'overall happiness' " (Dossey, *Time, Space and Medicine*, p. 63).

The effects of prayer as reframing are not limited, however, to restoring or maintaining health. Even more important for our purposes, prayer may effect an actual transformation of the central nervous system. The Kundalini experience in Tantric Hinduism and Buddhism is held to be just such a literal transformation of the organism. An Indian clerk for the water department, Gopi Krishna, has written a fascinating account of unexpectedly discovering powerful and painful physical effects after years of meditation. He lost appetite, weight, and strength from the sensation of fire within him. He described himself as near death before he discovered Sri Aurobindo, who explained the Kundalini phenomenon to him and guided him, not just back to health, but to reported dramatic increases in health, mental abilities, awareness, and parapsychological powers. In this country Lee Sanella has interviewed and collected case studies of persons with the Kundalini experience. Often they are unprepared for it and frightened by its onset. Even more unfortunately, they often fall into the hands of secular psychiatrists with even less understanding who drug them or have actually committed them to mental hospitals. Spiritual counselors are needed who have the background and experience to support persons through such crises that are at once spiritual and psychophysiological.

The point here is not to focus on these more dramatic cases. It is to emphasize that the prayer of discernment takes place, not just consciously, but as an actual transformation of the human organism in depth dialogue that reaches into the implicate order of the holoverse. Through reframing or changing the metaprograms we can connect to the holographic domain through the unconscious part of ourselves. The result is a healing of purpose that transforms the organism psychophysiologically. David Bohm, the theoretical physicist referred to at length in chapter 5 insists, "Meditation transforms the very structural matter of the brain" (Renee Weber, "The Enfolding-Unfolding Universe," a conversation with David Bohm, *ReVision* vol. 6, no. 1, p. 35).

This transformation is the depth work of the Holy Spirit which goes so far beyond our usual understanding of prayer as the conscious repetition of words. As noted above, Paul explains that the Spirit helps us with "sighs too deep for words." In the prayer of discernment, healing of purpose may come which literally changes our being and the world in which we live.

# CHAPTER EIGHT

# A New Metaphor: Can We Pray?

The three previous chapters have outlined the shifting of cultural beliefs that undergirded older metaphors for healing of purpose. What do we have to suggest in the light of those changes? We no longer operate in a culture in which it is assumed that we live and move and have our being in God. In a time of shifting and fragmentary beliefs, of rapid technological and social change, and of possible unprecedented planetary catastrophe, the fundamental question before us has to do with the reality and presence of God in human lives. People hunger to know, and ministers need to learn to affirm that presence and how to be in touch with God in their personal and corporate lives. We propose that the three historic metaphors for the healing of purpose be revitalized by a fundamental question for contemporary life: "Can we pray?"

At the same time, the question "Can we pray?" has more cultural support for its affirmative answer than at any time in Western history since at least before Newton. The chapter on the holoverse outlined an understanding of the fundamental nature of reality from modern physics that is remarkably like the testimony of mystics. The chapter on prayer in the holoverse described how prayer makes sense in that reality, supported by brain-mind research on the holographic functioning of the human mind. The previous chapter suggested that prayer can be understood as profound dialogue between conscious and unconscious, participating in God's literal transformation of us to become co-creators.

This chapter will outline the theory of a new metaphor for the healing of purpose based on worship, prayer, and meditation practice. The metaphor depends upon some very traditional understandings of prayer, enabling us to return to Augustine's central insight on transforming the will to love God. Through the ideas of the previous chapter, that transformation may be seen as dynamic growth rather than unremitting warfare against human desires. The metaphor enables us to escape from the linguistic ghetto, begun in Calvin's time and fully established with Dewey, in which religious faith gave up its confidence that it had to do with physical reality and human psychophysiology and contented itself with subjective experience and abstract discussion. The metaphor suggests that in the prayer of discernment, we are involved, not just in reshaping our linguistic metaphors of reality, but with the actual transformation of reality.

The metaphor focuses on how healing of purpose happens. God through Jesus Christ moves in our lives for healing as in the New Testament. The Christian community is the locus for the action of the Holy Spirit healing and empowering us for ministry. That healing and empowering happen in the prayer of discernment, in which we choose to participate in God's transforming grace in our lives. As Thomas Merton once wrote on the aim of spiritual direction, "As sons of God we are called to use our freedom *to help God create His likeness in our own soul. . . .* Our freedom, our love, our spontaneous contribution to God's work is itself the choicest and most precious effect of His grace" (*Spiritual Direction and Meditation*, p. 27). We have chosen to call that cooperative activity toward the healing of purpose the prayer of discernment. The chapter "Prayer in the Holoverse" described what prayer of discernment is.

The metaphor begins with the experience of men and women in the early centuries of the Christian church intending to live their lives in God. Among house congregations, urban basilicas, emerging monastic communities, and especially persons in solitude in the desert, a great amount of human experience and wisdom was developed about the quest. Specific practices such as the prayer of the heart were established in conjunction with a growing sense of stages or processes through which persons often pass in deepening their prayer life. Their experience and wisdom mark an important beginning point for exploring a metaphor for the healing of purpose based on the question, "Can we pray?" There is, however, a fundamental difficulty in accessing that wisdom from a very different cultural-historical situation. The desert mothers and fathers (and there were Ammas as well as Abbas) had a specific strategy for dealing with the social injustices and conflicts of their time. They fled from them. They went into the desert alone, to find God in their individual solitude.

Their solitude formed in the desert a holy counter-culture. Many of the sayings preserved from them detail the generosity, humility, and respect for each other's privacy that should obtain in their interpersonal relationships. Although not articulated as such, they endeavored to recreate the body of Christ in the desert—a community structured in all of its details with the single aim of living in the presence of God. Persons were transformed in that holy community, and sometimes, after many years, went back to the urban cultures of their time to witness to and transform them as well.

However, we tend to read the *Patrilogia*, the sayings from the desert, through the lens of the intervening centuries. Influenced by the mystical preoccupations of the great medieval and Catholic Counter-Reformation teachers, we are tempted to understand them as guides to individual paths to perfection. Influenced also by Renaissance and Enlightenment ideals of the autonomous individual, we assume spirituality to be a private adventure in the depths of the solitary individual, to which the community is a peripheral support. Given the ubiquitous influences of Gnosticism in the early centuries, in addition to the biases of more recent history, it is easy to do so.

In our time we struggle with social dimensions of our piety, how feminine and black and poor spirituality can confront and redeem what were thought to be universal understandings of faith but are now revealed to be at least partially white, middle-class, male European ones. We are beginning to understand how our prayer is an expression of the communities to which we belong as well as of our unique personal experience. One can read the desert mothers and fathers either way—as the story of the church as a holy community of voluntary poverty and shared solitude in God, or as the personal stories of men and women seeking God in their solitude and voluntary poverty. Both types of stories are true—either without the other is inadequate and misleading. Traditionally they have been read as lists of individual paths to sainthood, missing the dimension of community. But it is no better to read them only as a sociological case study and miss the dimension of personal experience.

Our attempt here will be to see them as wisdom about community formation *and* personal experience as well. Specifically I want to suggest that out of their teachings comes a simple, even crude, but useful map of the experience of prayer. The map can be thought of as three concentric circles; each one includes the previous ones. Each circle is a characterization of a specific type of community of prayer and a specific set of personal concerns about prayer. Each circle suggests certain types of prayer appropriate to it. Naming the three circles takes us back to early Christian history.

The Christian experience of the early centuries was articulated, among others, by the anonymous author of the works attributed to Dionysius the Pseudo-Areopagite. In this approach, the soul progresses by grace through the stages of purgation, illumination, and perfection or union (*Writings on Spiritual Direction by Great Christian Masters*, ed. Jerome M. Neufelder and Mary C. Coelho [New York: Seabury Press, 1982], p. 98). Purgation is the arduous and long process of cleansing the impurities, confusions, and distractions of one's life and ordering it according to the authority of the church and of God's commandments. It is especially concerned with overcoming pride and learning humility. Illumination is the stage by grace where discursive thought and prayer in the mode of active reflection give way to the community of contemplatives becoming quiet or still before God. Perfection or union is that rare admission to the kingdom of God achieved by very few where the soul lives continually in God. This simple and sturdy map has been used throughout Christian history from Saint Bonaventure to Evelyn Underhill. Each circle is thought to have types of prayer and meditation appropriate to it. Active reflective methods such as *lectio*, reading of scripture; *mediatio*, repetition of words or phrases from scripture; and examination of conscience, the twice-daily measuring of one's thoughts and actions against the standard of defined virtues, are especially useful in purgation. The use of affective prayer and contemplation increases in illumination, and the depths of contemplation—especially what is called passive infused contemplation—mark union.

Contemporary research on stages of faith development relates to this ancient map. Neill Hamilton has suggested that faith begins in discipleship in the church; meaning the confidence in one's human decision to follow Christ. An important example of discipleship in the gospels is the request of James and John for favored treatment in the kingdom of heaven. Jesus replies, "You do not know what you are asking. Are you able to drink the cup that I drink, or to be baptized with the baptism with which I am baptized?" (Mark 10:38). The two reply confidently, "We are able," not knowing, of course, what they are saying. Discipleship begins, according to Hamilton, with this simplistic and naïve act of human willing. He then suggests that the inescapable brokenness of life can bring about a "transition in spirit" through the experience of personal tragedy, failure or limitations, or the encountering of pain and suffering in the world. For those who grow to this point, acceptance and forgiveness by God lead to a new birth and a more profound understanding of the church and of following the risen Christ. The transition leads to the third stage of maturing in church and mission. In the church one sees one's interdependence in the body of Christ on the gifts distributed to all. In mission one witnesses to Christ and lives a life of ministering to others and working for social justice (Lectures by Neill Hamilton, Institute for Advanced Pastoral Studies, Southfield Mich., February 28–March 4, 1983).

James Fowler is perhaps the best known of a number of persons interested in research in faith development. Fowler builds on Lawrence Kohlberg's six stages of moral development in males, which in turn owe much to Jean Piaget's research on stages of cognitive development. Fowler suggests, following Kohlberg, that these stages are sequential, invariant, and irreversible, a true ladder of increasing sophisication, inclusiveness, and flexibility in understanding and living faith. He adds ideas from Jean Ricoeur on symbolic development or right-brain sophistication to Kohlberg's more left-brain ladder. His stage 3, conventional faith, has some connections to Hamilton's discipleship and even purgation. It is the stage of accepting and internalizing the faith of the family, school, church, and other collectives in which one lives. Like purgation, it is accepting the faith contexts of others. Like discipleship, it is a tacit, lived faith without a great deal of understanding or clear, conscious ownership. Stage 4, individuated faith, has some resemblances to illumination only in that it marks the achievement of autonomy. It is the clear

articulation of one's own beliefs regardless of the
teachings of the collective. In illumination one must
also go into one's own depths, and the discursive
teachings of the community must be left behind for
the authenticity of one's own lived experience.
Individuated faith is also related to Hamilton's
Transition in Faith in that it is also inaugurated by
breaking the earlier, simpler certainties. Fowler does
not emphasize the tragedies of life as much as the
inevitable rebellion against authority that the
achievement of autonomy requires. Fowler's stages 5
and 6, synthesizing and universalizing faith, seem to
blend somewhat together and bear some resemblances to Hamilton's maturing in faith in that they
attempt to describe the integration, awareness of
limitations, flexibility, self-giving, and transparency
that the saints among us seem to live. Like the
traditional stage of union, those who live at such a
level of universal community are rare indeed, and
perhaps difficult for the rest of us to comprehend.

These circles are not entered simply by individual
human willing, but by a complex enabling of
community formation, personal experience, and
most of all, by the grace of God. The author of *The
Cloud of Unknowing* warns against the novice's
thinking "that since he has given himself to prayer
and penance for a short time under the guidance of
his spiritual father, that he is now ready to begin
contemplation . . . He only imagines that grace is
calling him to contemplation . . . It is a straight path
to the death of body and soul, because it is a
perversion which leads to insanity. But he does not
recognize this and, foolishly thinking that he can
grasp God with his intellect alone, forces his mind to
focus on God alone" (*Writings on Spiritual Direction*,
pp. 104-5).

The following three chapters outline a simple threefold map for the healing of purpose under the names commitment, freedom, and compassion. I have attempted to characterize the community and personal experience of each circle, and then to suggest the characteristic forms of prayer appropriate to it. The three circles are meant to serve as a rough map of a metaphor for the healing of purpose based on the contemporary question, "Can we pray?"

# CHAPTER NINE

# Commitment

The first circle of prayer is *commitment*. Commitment happens when we love something or fear something enough to make a life-changing decision and act upon it. A friend of mine recently went through a very difficult funeral for an accidentally killed thirty-five-year-old man who was a friend and a member of his congregation. "He lived what I preached," my friend shared with me. Every once in a while we love a teacher or a friend or a spouse enough to change our lives. We clean up our act, not in order to please them, but because they disclose to us a new vision of who we can be and in fact are, in the image of God. Commitment is the first dimension of the healing of purpose. Alcoholics Anonymous and other self-help groups continue to demonstrate that the fear of what will happen or has happened if we don't change can also effectively motivate to life-changing commitment.

It is best if there is no reasonable alternative to the commitment. It is best to marry someone not because she ranks slightly higher than others on a ten-point scale, but because she is the only person I would want to spend the rest of my life with. I am apt to make such a life-changing commitment only when there is no other choice. Jesus asks the disciples after his hard sayings to them, "Will you also go away?" Peter responds, "Lord, to whom would we go? You have the words of eternal life." In the entryway to Japanese Buddhist Zendos, there are two steps on which the monks place their sandals when coming in from the outside. When persons wish to gain admittance to the community as a novice, they kneel on those steps in petition. There is no immediate answer. The postulant goes on kneeling while the Roshi and community, in seeming total indifference, go about their meditation and work. The postulant goes on kneeling as the morning of bright intention passes into the afternoon of stolid endurance and the night of hopelessness and despair. Still there is no sign that the community notices or cares, let alone welcomes its would-be newest member. But the postulant in stubborn persistence or desperation lasts out the night and begins the cycle of the second day of isolation and unrequited testing of will. Perhaps late in the next afternoon, the community, at last persuaded of the postulant's serious intent, relents and, through the person of the novice master, welcomes her into the community.

Something unique is required in each commitment—unique to the particular life situation and personality. We probably will avoid it and pretend a contentment we know is bogus. Probably the call will twist our hearts again and again, while we explain to our friends and to ourselves how we can have our good feelings and our self-deception too. If we are fortunate, the time will come when the God of fire and wrath begins to peek through the God of rosy sunsets. And we know in our guts that we are called to loss as well as gain, to sacrifice as well as abundance. Suddenly, after ignoring or floating through so many Holy Weeks, the collect cuts our hearts: "Almighty God, whose most dear son went not up to joy but first he suffered pain, and entered not into glory before he was crucified, mercifully grant . . ."

We are not ready for the end of the collect yet—we are still in the situation of the rich young man pondering the most unpleasant and unreasonable choice Jesus laid upon him. It is our choice—that's the damnable thing about it. Grace is absolutely free, and at the same time something is required of us. What it is is unique to each one. As Werner Erhard is fond of saying to an audience, "All you have to do is give up everything." Then he pauses, looks slyly around the room, and continues, "Actually you don't have to give up everything. All you have to give up is what you just thought of when I said to you—'You have to give up everything.' "

Commitment is lived through the ethical discipline of a community. In Theravada Buddhist practice the first stage toward enlightenment is *silla*—fulfilling the commandments. Before one has any possibility of progressing to higher stages of meditative practice, one must practice the eightfold path and learn to live in harmony, nonviolence and love toward, not just one's fellow human beings, but all living things. The practice of traditional Sikhs of wearing nets about the face to prevent the unwitting killing of insects by breathing them in becomes a poignant but totally understandable expression of the religious impulse to ethical discipline. Having our own hearts warmed and opened, how we can wittingly harm any other living thing that God creates and sustains?

Ethical discplines have many forms specific to the life situations of the communities who live them. The most profound formulation is the great commandment interpreted by Jesus from the Hebrew law: "You shall love the Lord your God with all your heart, and with all your soul, and with all your mind. This is the first and great commandment. And a second is like it; you shall love your neighbor as yourself. On these two commandments depend all the law and the prophets" (Matthew 22:37-40).

Ethical disciplines do not, in any ongoing religious community, stay on the level of abstract, though profound, generalization. They get translated and concretized into specific rules and regulations for daily routine and special circumstances. That is often irksome to the more free-spirited among us. But it is absolutely necessary for two reasons. First is the formation of the novice on the spiritual journey. The personal commitment is to a whole new life. Even if the particular first choice is clear, how does one construct a whole new life in God? What are all the ramifications of living in love instead of living for self? How ought one to go about the routines of daily life from a totally different perspective? How do we know if we are serious about the spiritual life or simply entertaining a new fad? *Formation* is a difficult but profound word—we need to be formed anew, and we need detailed guidance in all areas of our life to do that. And that is why the law of love must be translated into instructions for nutrition, interpersonal courtesies, or whatever the preoccupations of the particular tradition doing the translation.

There is a second and even more important reason for the specification of love into rules and commandments. It is to show the structure of reality. Before awakening, and the revelation that occasions it, we live in confusion. We are like a swimmer lost under cloudy water, swimming desperately even further from life because there is no clear way to go. Life itself presents no necessary order to reality, especially in these secular times. Some devote their lives to making money, others to even more immediate and egocentric pleasures. Some count their lives as failure and despair—others as happiness and success. And there doesn't seem to be much correlation between the life goals chosen and the satisfaction gained in pursuing them.

The light of awakening cuts through our confusions with a demand from reality. It turns out not to be true that life is some vague blob we can make of whatever we wish. There is someone out there and in there confronting us. There is after all some irreducible structure to life. We discover it just as we are about to shatter ourselves upon it, like waves on the Maine coast. Well, then, what is the structure?

The answer, like all things in the human condition, is never written unambiguouly in the sky in a universal language. Structure there is, and unalterable consequence for our actions. But we must discover it by the most inadequate of tools which bend and shatter in our hands before that hard rock. We are working in the dark as well, at least as badly off as Plato's prisoners, attempting to disentangle reality from the human illusion. And we do not even have a sure way of recordng our findings so that we might pass them on to our children. The psalmist prays:

Teach me, O Lord, the way of thy statutes
and I will keep it to the end.
Give me understanding that I may keep thy law
and observe it with my whole heart.
Lead me in the path of thy commandments,
for I delight in it.

Psalm 119:33-35

We cherish the law when it comes. It is our hearts' desire to know God. The law is the method, the way to God our heart desires. It is the best we know of the structure of reality, given by revelation, cherished and corrupted by tradition.

That is why, among other reasons, the church exists. Each church tradition has, over the generations of its existence, developed its own ways of doing things. Those ways are not always conscious, even to the leaders of the community, and the most important tips and clues are not written down in books. They are instead resident in the minds and hearts of the members and teachers of the community. Michael Polanyi is the philosopher of science who has written most profoundly that every scientific field or academic discipline is a function of the community of practitioners in which it is incarnated:

> Tacit assent and intellectual passions, the sharing of an idiom and of a cultural heritage, affiliation to a like minded community: such are the impulses which shape our vision of the nature of things and on which we rely for the mastery of things. No intelligence, however critical or original, can operate outside such a fiduciary framework. (Michael Polanyi, *Personal Knowledge: Towards a Post-Critical Philosophy* [New York: Harper Torchbooks, 1958], p. 266)

One becomes a physicist not by reading books, but by learning to "act like a physicist" as an apprentice in the community of physicists. The learning takes place at all levels of being, conscious and unconscious. In the same way, we learn and internalize our Christian faith through participating in the Christian community.

Commitment comes through a dialectic of authority and personal decision. There is an intrinsic authority and power in the root insights of the community and tradition. It is clear that we did not, could not, invent them ourselves solely from our experience in this life in this culture in this time. When not rebellious or attempting the magic of literalism, we are genuinely humbled and transformed as we stand before those insights. It is not that they are simply very wise, and we were not clever enough to think of them; it is that they are symbolic avenues of relationship between ourselves and the God who we are not.

Commitment is the life-changing decision we act upon. It is a curious paradox of confidence in one's human will and ability to change one's life lived in dependence upon someone else's rules, the ethical discipline of the church community. The phenomenon of the "new Christian" in our time illustrates that the committed ones are not always pleasant to live with. They have newly discovered the law of love and are quite self-confident of their ability to live it and sometimes intolerant of those who have to struggle with more complex issues of faith. Their commitment is a life-changing human possibility by dint of serious dedication and hard work.

The prayer of discernment has appropriate forms for commitment. The forms have to do first of all with reflection. The secularized, idiosyncratic psyche needs to be filled with Christian concepts, images, structures, and processes. Theology as cognitive understanding, corporate liturgy, structured forms of personal prayer, and contemporary versions of examination of conscience are needed. Persons newly committed need to learn how to pray. Traditional introductions to prayer are appropriate but may be stale or irrelevant to persons in contemporary culture and need to be adapted. For example, a stereotyped examination of conscience may be meaningless, but an introduction to journal writing may be very exciting.

Types of reflection are so well known that I wish here to focus on the second essential form of prayer in commitment—contemplation. Contemplation is the basic training of prayer and meditation. Just as an athlete needs to train his or her body for deep involvement in sports, so a Christian needs to train mind and body for the disciplines of prayer and meditation. Contemplation is a way of doing this. The simplest way to describe contemplation is a full attention or presence in the here and now. Most of us spend much of our time worrying about the future, regretting the past, and being somewhere else instead of here. Contemplation is the skill training by which we begin to be right here and right now, able to pay attention to the present—to what is, to what is happening.

It is like falling in love. Life no longer runs its accustomed course because she intrudes. Her face, her name, something she said, or the way she looked unexpectedly pops up into conciousness, and the task I was in the midst of no longer seems very important. Or I suddenly realize that I have been staring out the window for some time now, riding a crest of golden feeling, totally unaware of my environment. When I am not otherwise occupied, she fills my mind, and it is only with difficulty that I push her out to do what needs to be done next. I begin to see the rest of my world in relation to her. I create stories and vignettes from it to delight her. I learn new ways of seeing when I am with her that profoundly affect how I view the rest of my life. She so attracts me that everything else is lived in relationship and reference to that central pole of my love for her. She unbalances my universe. It seems to me that I am continually boring my friends with conversation about her. My motivation for everything other than being with her diminishes in a frightening way. I begin to question my mental status and whether I can continue to live in this volcano of emotions. I finally admit it to myself—I am obsessed with her. This is contemplation; or more precisely, that is the experience of contemplation: the focusing of one's whole being on the single point of one's commitment.

The aim of contemplation is the fusion of intention or decision and receptiveness or awareness. One learns through practice what it is like to totally attend to something without effort or striving. How do we learn to do this? If we try it, we quickly learn the first lesson—one cannot manipulate the mind directly into silence and focus. If we try, for example, not to think of red Volkswagens for three minutes, they immediately pop up into consciousness. If we try to forcefully shut out all distracting thoughts so we can be at peace, they intrude from everywhere. If we tell ourselves not to worry about that argument with our child, in the next instant we realize we are rehearsing how we wish we had related to him.

The mind requires gentleness and indirectness in training. There is no use pushing ourselves around— we just make ourselves unhappy and dispirited. The great religious traditions agree that an indirect strategy is necessary. That strategy has literally

hundreds of different forms—but the essential principle is the same. We give the mind a simple repetitive
stimulus to rest on. For example, it can be the blue of a
candle's flame. We look at it without staring or trying
to concentrate. When our mind wanders, we very
gently include the blue of the flame back into our
consciousness. We let our consciousness rest there
without forcing or judging ourselves or feeling guilty
when our attention falters. This is how we learn
contemplation, to be here and now, focusing on the
names God gives us for our commitment.

Why do all of this? What does it have to do with
commitment? Contemplation has, of course, very
specific practical advantages. Stilling the mind profoundly relaxes one, allows the body's natural processes of healing to operate, and clears the mind for
wiser decision making. There is now scientific literature on the benefits of contemplation. One among
many books is *The Mind/Body Effect* by Herbert
Benson (New York: Simon & Schuster, 1979). In
Japan, business executives and athletes will study at a
Buddhist Zendo for what is called Bompo Zen. They
have no interest in the religious practice as such. They
are there to learn to become more effective in their
work and play. And contemplation accomplishes that.

But that is not the reason contemplation is discussed
here. Contemplation is necessary for the prayer of
discernment. In attempting to live our commitment,
we sense the difference between our distracted
egocentric lives and what God calls us to. We cannot
bridge that difference by acts of will and good
intentions alone. We need to learn how to go toward
God. Contemplation is the inward discipline by which
we learn how to do that. It is the aspect of the prayer of
discernment by which we first learn how to put aside
our old lives and take on the new life of Christ.

## CHAPTER TEN

# Freedom

The brokenness of life, as Hamilton suggests, overwhelms commitment and occasions the second dimension of growth in prayer which is called freedom. Commitment to living the law of love contains the seeds of its own transcendence, because the law cannot be fulfilled by unaided human will. That is the great message of Paul; that the law brings us to the conviction of sin that we might be open to the grace of God in Jesus Christ.

If it had not been for the law, I should have not known sin. I should not have known what it is to covet if the law had not said, 'You shall not covet.' But sin, finding opportunity in the commandment, wrought in me all kinds of covetousness. Apart from the law sin lies dead. I was once alive apart from the law, but when the commandment came, sin revived and I died; the very

159

> commandment which promised life proved to be death
> to me. . . . Who will deliver me from this body of death?
> Thanks be to God through Jesus Christ our Lord!
> (Romans 7:7-10, 24b-25a)

The experience of the futility of will is usually not a
falling away from the life or prayer but the result of
deepening it. As we see more deeply into our own
hearts and experience more keenly the suffering of
others through our greater sensitivity to them, the
simpler verities of commitment are insufficient. As
noted above, it is not a conscious decision on our part
that brings us to this dimension. It is the accumu-
lated weight of our experience that bears us deeper.
We usually resist it because it seems to be a falling
away from faith rather than a deepening faith. Saint
Teresa of Avila complained about the spiritual
directors of her time who had not experienced this
crisis and deepening in their own lives and therefore
resisted and retarded it in those who came to them.
"Let seculars give thanks to God that they can choose
their own director, and let them not give up that
previous liberty, but rather remain without one until
they find the one whom the Lord will give" (Kenneth
Leech, *Soul Friend* [London: Sheldon Press, 1977], p.
66). Saint John of the Cross "particularly attacks
those directors who are ignorant of contemplative
prayer and who therefore urge their unfortunate
disciples to greater efforts in meditation (*meditatio*),
'They know no way with souls but to hammer and
batter them like a blacksmith' " (ibid.).

At some point we have to go it alone. Not isolated
from church and scripture and those who love us, but
not depending upon them for the work that only we
can do. Robertson Davies in *Manticore* through Liesl

counsels David, who is considering whether or not to continue a second year of Jungian analysis:

> Analysis with a great analyst is an adventure in self-exploration. [She then comments on the greatness of Freud, Adler, and Jung.] All men of extraordinary character, and they devised systems that are forever stamped with that character. . . . Davey, did you ever think that these three men who were so splendid at understanding others had first to understand themselves? It was from their self-knowledge they spoke. They did not go trustingly to some doctor and follow his lead because they were too lazy or too scared to make the inward journey alone. They dared heroically. And it should never be forgotten that they made the inward journey while they were working like galley-slaves at their daily tasks, considering other people's troubles, raising families, living full lives. They were heroes, in a sense that no space-explorer can be a hero, because they went into the unknown absolutely alone. Was their heroism meant to raise a whole new crop of invalids? Why don't you go home and shoulder your yoke, and be a hero, too? (Robertson Davies, *Manticore* [New York: Penguin Books, 1972], pp. 265-66)

Each of us must learn to become a patient empirical investigator, an expert in exploring our own inner experience. Freud once compared himself to a spelunker—an explorer of caves—going deeper and further into the caverns of the human psyche than anyone had ever dared to go before. Each one of us committed to serious prayer and meditation practice is such a spelunker—going patiently deeper and further into our own experience than we have ever dared to go before. In doing so, time and time again we will be forced, if we are to be true to our experience, to radically revise our own cherished beliefs. Our vocation is to be a specialist in the field of our own experience.

We must find the paradoxical courage, by grace, to see ourselves nonjudgmentally, in the light of the law and in our own uniqueness. With the patience and dispassionate observation of a skilled empirical investigator, which we are or will become if we persist, we are to look into the depths—denying nothing that is there, pretending nothing to be there that is not, always pressing on toward the goal of insight and transformation we cannot have even imagined beforehand. "Beloved, we are God's children now; it does not yet appear what we shall be, but we know that when he appears we shall be like him, for we shall see him as he is" (I John 3:2).

It is said that there are three requirements for rigorous practice in Rinzai Zen Buddhism: a great root of faith, a great ball of doubt, and great tenacity of purpose. And so it must be with us scientists of the inner realm. "Isn't that interesting—I am simply sitting here quietly and I am in terror for my life." "Now that's worth looking at—I am in such great bliss I cannot find words to describe it, and my heart feels as if it is pouring forth tears of compassion." "Now this is remarkable—I am so bored sitting here it is only with every last ounce of my will, and then just a pinch more, that I am able to persist."

This process is not introspection understood in its usual way—as analyzing oneself. We are not involved in trying to figure out why we are thinking or feeling something. We are dispassionately exploring what is. Another of Werner Erhard's aphorisms: "The question 'Why?' will drive you insane; the question 'What?' will drive you sane."

In the dimension of freedom, we are forced to give up taking ourselves on someone else's terms, even those of the best authority. As Fowler emphasizes, it is a time of owning our own autonomy through intimate acquaintance with our own experience. At this point traditional teachings on prayer give way to the risk and fear and excitement of trusting our own experience, no matter to what frightening places it may seem to lead us. Only long and careful discipline in the dimension of commitment gives a secure and sound enough ego structure, supportive relationships, and ethical life-style for this part of the journey. For when it is undertaken, no prior securities can be counted upon.

In the process we may literally reach beneath our usual sensory experience to the holographic functioning of our organism. For example, the experience of inner sounds or music is recorded in some mystical literature. There is held to be the actual hearing of musical sounds after long practice in meditation. Far from being hyperbole or nonsense, recent research indicates that it may be the direct experience of the holographic functioning of the ear. The ear evidently generates "its own reference beam, or 'reference silence.' It is the interference between external sounds and the reference sound that provides the brain with spatial information" (*Brain-Mind Bulletin* 8, no. 10 [May 30, 1983], p. 1). The reference sound works just as the laser beam does in the visual hologram. It is possible to record this sound directly from the ear, and scientists have done so. Tinnitus is the pathological condition in which the sounds are so loud the person is oppressed by them and which commonly accompanies deafness. But the sounds also emanate more softly constantly from normal, healthy ears. "They are fairly complex with regard to frequency, a sort of background hum with well defined pure tones or whistles superimposed" (ibid., p. 2).

The dimension of freedom takes one deeply into the cloud of forgetting in which the old categories are left behind. From moral certainties to the awareness of our moral ambiguities, from conscious to unconscious, from sensory experience to holographic reality, freedom leads to the miracle of God's love beneath phenomenal experience. But the miracle of God's glory is not an exception or a freakish occurrence to reality; it is the way things really are. Blake's poem I learned in high school suggests the miracle is there in every detail of the world, if we could only see it.

> To see the World in a grain of sand,
> And a Heaven in a wild flower,
> Hold Infinity in the palm of your hand,
> And Eternity in an hour . . .

The miracle is *not* supernatural, whatever that Latin abstraction means. The miracle is the truly *natural*. It is the way things really are if we could just see it. We experience the inner world the same way we experience the outer world—through our senses: sight, hearing, touch on the skin and inside the body, smell and taste. These are our necessary and only connections to lived reality. But they are not automatic objective sensors that report things the way they really are. They operate the way we have unwittingly taught them to. They hold our world steady and consistent because that is the way we have been taught to create our world. When we see a new face, it "reminds us of . . ." Every new precept is jammed into the old coding systems as best we can. "Don't worry, dear, it's just a dream." "Oh, that's just a . . ." One evening I saw *Blow Up* with some friends in a strange city. The film plays with changing perceptions of illusion and reality through a greatly enlarged photograph unwittingly taken of a murder in progress. When I went outside the theater afterward, the first thing I saw was a clock atop the city hall. Only the clock had no hands. Turning a corner we were confronted with police barriers across the sidewalk, blocking our way. But there were no police, no crowds, no construction in progress; no ostensible reason for their presence. They were just there. Next, fire trucks came rushing past with sirens at full volume, no fires in sight—no context for their presence in that quiet Midwestern night. Suddenly I realized that Antonioni's surrealism had temporarily become my world too—and I was perceiving reality in its context. The clock without hands, the mysterious police barriers, the unexplained fire trucks—I did not invent them; I discovered them in external reality. And I indeed had created that reality after the movie's for a few moments.

Life does imitate art—the artwork of the world we have created. Even the way we perceive, touch, hear, see is part of that artwork. The senses are, in Brugh Joy's term—a *scaffolding* (W. Brugh Joy, *Joy's Way* [Los Angeles: J. P. Tarcher, 1979], p. 6). We perceive inner and outer reality by means of them, and we have unwittingly shaped the way we perceive by means of them. Then, in the moment of awareness, the scaffolding drops away, and we "see." With transformed senses, or beyond sensory perception, we are directly aware, "in touch" with reality.

And that reality is remarkably different from the reality we have been socialized to observe. Not opposite, just different—as if it exists in a different dimension, foreign from our accustomed experience. We have both the authoritative findings of modern physics and the testimony of ancient mystics to assure us that is the case. Out of fatigue we stare at the variegated rug. After a while we notice the rug

beginning to heave slightly, then sway and move. We
start to become dizzy, break the stare, and remind
ourselves that the apparent movement is simply an
illusion caused by the circulation of blood vessels
behind the retina.

But is it illusion? On the contrary, the illusion is
that the rug is a steady, solid object. In reality it and
we are a shimmering dance of energy fields in a
space-time continuum with quarks and baryons
appearing and disappearing and transforming into
each other in endless movement. We hold fast the
illusion that we are permanent and the rug is steady
so we can get about the business of living in
conventional society, not because that is the way
things are.

Mystics are, or should be, simply folk who are more
curious about seeing what is really there than most of
us are. And what they report, at least in some
traditions, when they become more deeply aware, is
of "things arising and passing away." They *experience*
what physicists find in their experiments. What the
mystics experience is not another reality, cast in the
same mold as conventional reality, but of a different
color or shape or whatever. That is the problem with
the word *supernatural*. It suggests another world on
top of or better than this one, but fundamentally of
the same order. What mystics experience is the
breaking of the limits of experiencing. Karl Jaspers
called the mystical events "boundary situations"
(Karl Jaspers, *Philosophy*, trans. E. B. Ashton
[Chicago: University of Chicago Press, 1979]). They
cross or transcend the boundary of everyday experiencing into . . . what?

Certainly not to another world—a sort of techni-
color Oz in the sky. Heaven is not Plato set for
television, in spite of the fantasies of some traditional

Christian piety. The breakthrough to full awareness is the dropping away of sensory resources into . . . There are no words for it precisely because it is beyond words—although mystics have habitually used metaphors and allegories to describe it, piling up archangels upon angels, and indulging in whatever hyperbole came to mind. The best words are pairs of contradictions, i. e., luminous darkness, plenum and void. They indicate the boundaries of sensory experience, the awesome direct awareness of reality as such, unmediated by the particulars of the phenomenal world. To see the world in a grain of sand is to see the world, the fullness of God's universe, shining through one perceived detail of that universe. At moments even the peceived detail drops away and we experience the whole directly. "Pure consciousness without an object," "reality as such," "ground of being," "not this, not that." Such abstractions may or may not be useful to hint at the experience. Negative pointers to the true nature of reality seem best. In the Christian tradition this is termed *apophatic theology*. Apophatic theology is the theology of negatives which takes away descriptions of God to uncover the nameless mystery.

Seeing the holographic nature of reality changes my self-understanding as well. It enables me to let go of my fixed self-images and see myself, as well as the world, continually arise and pass away, a continual fresh creation of God in every moment. A name for the first enlightenment in Japanese Buddhist practice is *Kensho*. It means insight into the true nature of the self. A characteristic contemplation aid to occasion that insight is:

At this very moment
Thinking neither of good nor of evil

What was your original face
Before your parents were born?

The "answer" is not in words but in seeing that the true nature of our self comes fresh from the hand of God in every moment. There is no permanent self any more than there is a permanent world. Job suffers many losses and personal tragedies without cause or explanation. Pastoral counselors come to him and patiently explain that he must have done something wrong. If he would just confess it, he could manipulate God into restoring his fortunes and guaranteeing the permanent survival of his separate self. But Job will have none of it. He knows that he is broken and that no amount of self-repair, especially on a deceitful basis, will help. Then it is recorded that God appears before Job, rising out of the whirlwind, and challenging him: "Who is this that darkens counsel by words without knowledge? Gird up your loins like a man, I will question you, and you shall declare to me. Where were you when I laid the foundations of the earth? Tell me, you have understanding" (Job 38:2-4).

God's challenge is not a way to humiliate Job. It is a profound invitation to remember his true nature—that he is created afresh from God in every moment and, therefore, in eternity. As a warrior, he needs no righteous or guilty self to cling to, only continual offering to and receiving from God. George Leonard suggests that the human condition is that we are at one and the same time an absolutely unique creation and an undifferentiated manifestation of the universe (*The Silent Pulse* [New York: E. P. Dutton, 1978]). We are both unique I's and simple aspects of God's love. The dialectic is logically contradictory; it is also the way we really are. To come to freedom is to leave behind the striving for a permanent fixed self. "Freedom," goes the song "Me and Bobby McGee," "is just another word for nothing left to lose."

The dark night of Saint John of the Cross sums up the moral and mystical aspects of freedom. There are three stages to the darkness. The first is the darkness of privation. The senses and the desires lose their power; even the bliss of earlier prayer experiences is withdrawn. The will becomes powerless to make prayer satisfying as commitment. Then comes the darkness of faith. The boundaries of commitment, of self and God, of our ability to understand, to make sense out of our experience, also disappear into the night. Finally, as we come too close to direct experience of divine reality, the darkness of God comes upon us. For, "the clearer the light the more it blinds and darkens the eye of the soul; and the more directly one looks at the sun, the greater the darkness and privation it causes to the visual faculty" (Leech, *Soul Friend*, p. 161). Thus,

> these three parts of the night are all one night; but like night itself it has three parts. For the first part, which is that of sense, is compared to the beginning of night, the point of which things begin to fade from sight. And the second part which is faith is comparable to midnight which is total darkness. And the third part is like the close of night which is God, the which part is now near to the light of day. (Ibid., p. 160)

The approach or styles of prayer appropriate to freedom are those called in certain traditions contemplative prayer. Here we have used the word *contemplation* for the first dimension of commitment and *meditation* for those deeper states of freedom. Meditation is the breakthrough that comes in the depth of contemplation. Contemplation is skill

training. Meditation is the free, instantaneous awareness of reality by grace, usually after long, patient
discipline. We can will to contemplate. We cannot
will to meditate. Meditation is the fruit of our
discipline, wrought by grace, experienced in freedom, coming in our practice and daily living, often
when we least expect it. It is the breakthrough to full,
unmediated awareness of what is, things arising and
passing away. Meditation passes through the scaffolding of words and of the senses to direct seeing.
Who sees? God sees/we see. God creates in seeing. We
become co-creators in seeing.

Meditation seems to have two forms. The reflection
of commitment means to fill the psyche with a
storehouse of Christian images, thoughts, feelings,
and behavior patterns. Reflection gives way to
insight in meditation, as in freedom we become able
to look more directly at what is there in the depths,
not what we wish were there or believe should be
there. We discover "strange beasts and have unique
adventures" as Auden suggests. We encounter our
"besetting sin" or favorite demon who will not let us
go, or whom we will not let go; wrestling not just one
night as Jacob did, but weary and despairing months
and years. Through dreams, through long and patient
silence, through the joy and suffering of life, the
panorama of inner reality gradually comes into view
and begins to disentangle itself from our naïve
projection of it onto others and the world. The
unconscious and conscious mind become intimate
friends and adversaries rather than strangers.

The second form of meditation is the surprising
moments of mystical insight when we see the
seamless whole of reality. The holoverse is no longer
hidden by sensory experience, but by grace we are in
God's love, out of which we see the universe created

and dissolved and created anew in every instant.

These forms of meditation cannot be taught as skills, like reflection or contemplation. We wait upon God patiently, in silence and prayer, for the deepening. If there is any act of will, it is the paradoxical one of letting go. In Philippians, Paul, exhorting the members of the church to love one another, describes letting go as self-emptying.

> Let each of you look not only to his own interests, but also to the interests of others. Have this mind among yourselves, which is yours in Christ Jesus, who, though he was in the form of God, did not count equality with God a thing to be grasped, but emptied himself, taking the form of a servant, being born in the likeness of men. And being found in human form, he humbled himself and became obedient unto death, even death on the cross (Philippians 2:4-9)

Letting go is both an emptying and a filling which go on simultaneously.

The emptying is the letting go of the images by which we believe the rest of the world or some significant part of it is an extension of ourselves. Or to be more precise, of our ego.

We begin life simply as an unselfconscious, undifferentiated part of our environment. Growth entails differentiation, i. e., becoming aware that we are not the same as our environment and taking responsibility for our self as an increasingly autonomous entity acting freely in relation to that environment. The process is experienced as both gain and loss. We gain a sense of power as we realize that we are free and can affect our environment by our actions and that we are not just an expression of the will of our parents or family, but that we have something to say about what goes on. Differentiation

is also experienced as loss—the loss of security—and
dependency on others. Often the painful sense of loss
is more poignant and controlling than the liberating
sense of power and freedom; and we choose to stay
undifferentiated even in an oppressive environment
rather than risk the aloneness, separation, and
responsibility for one's own selfhood that differentiation brings.

Up to a certain point the culture supports our
efforts at freedom, then it is indifferent to or opposes
them. Leaving home and rebelling against family
values are highly approved. There is even an old
American value that the children should surpass the
parents. That does not mean that letting go of family
attachments and identifications is simple or easy. In
fact most of us much of the time unwittingly go
around putting our parents' faces on our co-workers,
spouses, and friends and acting out the early family
dramas over and over again. The names have been
changed, but the plots remain the same. If a person
goes even further to question or disidentify with the
economic order or values taught by the culture about
making money, those around him are puzzled and
upset. They are upset because by disidentifying with
cultural values, the person by implication questions
and threatens the structures of psychic security
others have so carefully built up and maintained.
Seldom were the Pharisees so hostile to Jesus as when
he disidentified from their mechanical loyalty to
carefully worked out rules by which to live every
aspect of their lives. "The sabbath was made for man,
not man for the sabbath" (Mark 2:27) was and is an
outrageous disidentification with the specifics of
Hebrew law in favor of autonomous decision making
based on love.

Letting go is a decision to dissolve, empty out, a

particular image that is part of my identity and
psychic security. Our psyche is cluttered with such
images and ego ideals which keep our lives predict-
able when things get confused, and which give us
some handles to assure us who we are when the night
anxiety comes on. They are all part of the baggage we
packed when we left Eden to armor our vulnerability
and to defend against our nakedness. Letting go does
not just mean relaxing, although that is a helpful
preliminary step. It means giving up the images and
ego ideals by which we defend against the terror of
unpremeditated freedom to create who we are in
every moment. All of us have emptying to do. That
includes our attachments to our childhood misfortunes, our definitions of success, our desires to keep
the world just the way it is so we can be safe, our
hatreds, our personal history, even our images of our
body. Only as we let go of the illusions that these
symbols control and determine us are we free to take
responsibility as autonomous selves for our family,
our vocation, our personal history, our bodies.
Self-emptying has no limit, only the invitation to give
up whatever is impeding us now.

Jesus in his life, death, and resurrection is our
model of what self-emptying is about. In Gethse-
mane, in his agony of tears like great drops of blood
falling to the earth, he experiences his pain at losing
all he held dear. God knows what that all was; surely
the teachings committed to his disciples, the women
who followed him and have no way of keeping alive
apart from the community he had established, the
tax collectors who now also have no means of
livelihood, the beauty of sunrise across the Sea of
Galilee, the quiet pleasure of walking among olive
trees at twilight, those dear friends whose lives are
irrevocably bound to his own, the sheer joy of being

alive. He grieves them all openly and honestly. "Nevertheless, not my will but yours be done." As Jesus let go of the prerogatives of Godhead in the incarnation, so he now also chooses to let go of the glories and small satisfactions of being human in the crucifixion.

Letting go is a filling as well as an emptying. For when the attachments clear out, we are free to be filled with the fullness of the love of God. Here we go beyond the possibility of words to help us much, as mentioned earlier. In a letter to Corinth, Paul confesses his inability to find words to report his mystical experience. The great religious traditions have strained the resources of art and communication to report what a God-filled life looks like. The miracle comes by grace to the empty heart. "Blessed are you that hunger now," Jesus promises in his compassion, "for you shall be satisfied" (Luke 6:21).

# CHAPTER ELEVEN

# Compassion

Compassion completes commitment and freedom and is the culmination of the healing of purpose. It is the way we become co-creators with God, as our skewed and partial purposes are reached and healed in God's love. In the prayer of discernment we touch into the implicate order of the holoverse, united with and transformed by the wisdom and compassion of the whole. In the prayer of discernment the church actualizes that larger purpose in specific actions in mission and ministry. In that prayer the healing of purpose happens as we decide to follow God's larger call for us and for the creation. The prayer of discernment reaches below the level of sensory experience to the fundamental reality of the holoverse. But this transcending the boundaries of conventional reality is not primarily a matter of breakthrough in sensory perception. It is fundamentally a matter of the heart, not of the senses. Our eyes and our ears open because our heart opens. The method of the mystic is analogous to the method of the physicist in rigor and in findings, but the aim is very different. The aim of the mystic and of the prayer of discernment is love: to express the loving purpose of God in this human life and this world.

Love, according to the Christian gospel, is what God is about. Therefore, according to the same gospel, love is what we are to be about. Love completes the dimensions of commitment and freedom. By commitment we take charge of our lives and our actions in the world. We receive through commitment intimations from God that the world is not random chaos, but an arena for purposeful activity to bring all things to God. As we mature in our commitments and participation in God's mission in the world, we come to moments of freedom when the creation becomes transparent, and the bright epiphany of God's direct and immediate presence shines through phenomenal reality. Then we see that God is all in all, in all things arising and passing away. In those moments of meditation we realize that reality is infinitely more marvelously magical than any supernatural expectations we could have manufactured. We are truly surprised by God and know that in the ultimate sense there are no limits—all things are possible for those who love God, who are called according to God's promise.

Following commitment and freedom, compassion is the third act in the drama of prayer and meditation practice. It brings us back to our beginning—to the concrete reality of the world and our human condition. Commitment is heroic. It is the way we take charge of our lives and our world, to order them

closer to our and God's hearts' desires. In freedom,
direct and immediate meditation is mystical. We see
beyond and beneath the clutter of this life, to true
reality, and we return with stars in our eyes. Neither
heroes nor dreamers are fully human, for they both
tinker with lived reality—heroes to change it,
dreamers to see beyond it. Lovers alone are fully
human. For they are in love with what is, and love it
back to God. The dimension of compassion might be
called Love II. It goes beyond the good intentions of
Love I as understood in commitment to a surrender
of the will and a more gentle and vulnerable
expression of God's love. As purpose is healed, it
becomes more graceful and less forceful. Compassion
includes and goes beyond commitment and freedom.
It comes back to the world. Buddhist practice is full
of enigmatic statements that the end of enlightenment is to come back to the beginning.

> Before enlightenment,
> chopping wood and carrying water
> after enlightenment,
> chopping wood and carrying water

There is a fantastic difference, of course—the
difference between being trapped by one's own
survival anxieties in the world of daily routine and
loving all living beings in that world for their own
sake, to bring them to the fulfillment of their promise.
The summary statement of that insight is "*Nirvana* is
*samsara.*" *Nirvana*, the final enlightenment, is *samsara,* the created order of cause and effect. The
ox-herding pictures in Zen practice are a series of ten
drawings in which the ox is the metaphor for
universal mind or the true nature of reality, and the
peasant is the hero or journeyer who wishes to find

and tame the ox. In the first picture the peasant is alone, separated from the ox, but intent upon finding it. In subsequent frames the peasant sees the tracks of the ox, finds it, grabs its halter, mounts it to ride and tame it, and finally merges with the ox as symbol of universal mind. This stage is usually depicted by no visual image at all—only white paper, or an empty circle. But this is not the end of the process. For the final frame shows the happy peasant returning to the marketplace and everyday life. He has come full circle—from separation to union and now back to everyday life from where he started. But that "final" stage is simply the ongoing process, depending on the circles or spirals of spirtual deepening which have gone before, are in process now, and are yet to come. Love brings the two worlds together—the world of everyday reality and the world of mystic visions. Compassion *sees* them intersect, and in doing so creates the miracle.

*Journey to Ixtlan* is the third volume of Carlos Castaneda's remarkable anthropological and spiritual journey with the teacher he calls Don Juan. In this book he comes to the culmination of his apprenticeship as a warrior or man of knowledge. Don Juan refuses to teach or explain any more to him and sends him alone into the "friendly mountains." In his journey in the desert he "talks to" a magic coyote, sees the luminous "lines of the world," and senses his mysterious "ally." On his return he recounts all that has happened to him, and Don Juan, with "obvious interest," comments, "You have simply *stopped the world.*" He goes on to explain that in stopping the world Carlos has broken through his cultural conditioning and experienced the "seeing between the worlds" which is the mark of the warrior or man of knowledge.

"Yesterday the world became as sorcerers tell you it is,"
he went on. "In that world coyotes talk and so do deer, as
I once told you, and so do rattlesnakes and trees and all
other living beings. But what I want you to learn is
SEEING. Perhaps you know now that SEEING happens
only when one sneaks between the worlds, the world of
ordinary people and the world of sorcerers. You are now
smack in the middle point between the two. Yesterday
you believed the coyote talked to you. Any sorcerer who
doesn't SEE would believe the same, but one who SEES
knows that to believe that is to be pinned down in the
realm of sorcerers. By the same token, not to believe that
coyotes talk is to be pinned down in the realm of
ordinary men." (Carlos Castaneda, *Journey to Ixtlan*
[New York: Pocket Books, 1972], p. 254)

To be born anew to the kingdom of God is to love, to
see between the worlds. It is the culmination of
prayer and meditation practice, the promise of grace,
and the fruit of our discipline. Upon his return from
the desert, Jesus returns to his hometown of Nazareth
to begin his public ministry. In the synagogue on the
sabbath, he announces that ministry by reading from
Isaiah: "The spirit of the Lord is upon me, because he
has anointed me to preach good news to the poor. He
has sent me to proclaim release to the captives and
recovering of sight to the blind, to set at liberty those
who are oppressed, to proclaim the acceptable year of
the Lord!" (Luke 4:18-19).

That passage proclaims the coming of the kingdom
of God into the midst of the changes and circumstances of this life. The incarnation embodies and
symbolizes the reign of God, transforming and
redeeming this world and our lives here and now.

In love our smaller purposes are healed or
redeemed in the larger purposes of God which are
infinitely beyond our conscious understanding and
the efficacy of our will. Love begins and ends in

mystery. It is above all the dimension of life and practice we can neither control nor totally understand with our intellect. That is because love is the profound depth of relationship human beings can ever live with the God who creates, sustains, and redeems us. Carl Jung said these very wise words about love toward the end of his life:

> Whatever one can say, no words express the whole. To speak of partial aspects is always too much or too little, for only the whole is meaningful. Love "bears all things" and "endures all things." Corinthians 1:13-7 These words say all there is to be said; nothing can be added to them. For we are in the deepest sense the victims and the instruments of cosmogonic "love." I put the word in quotation marks to indicate that I do not use it in its connotations of desiring, preferring, favoring, wishing, and similar feelings, but as something superior to the individual, a unified and undivided whole. Being a part, man cannot grasp the whole. He is at its mercy. He may assent to it, or rebel against it, but he is always caught up by it and enclosed within it. He is dependent upon it and sustained by it. Love in his light and his darkness, whose end he cannot see. "Love ceases not"—whether he speaks with the "tongues of angels," or with scientific exactitude traces the life of the cell down to its uttermost source. Man can try to name love, showering upon it all the names at his command, and still he will involve himself in endless self deceptions. If he possesses a grain of wisdom, he will lay down his arms and name the unknown by the more unknown, *ignotum per ignotis*— that is, by the name God. That is a confession of his subjection, his imperfection, and his dependence; but at the same time a testimony to his freedom to choose between truth and error. (C. G. Jung, *Memories, Dreams, Reflections*, ed. Amela Jaffe [New York: Pantheon, 1963], p. 354)

Living out the prayer of discernment as compassion does not mean to have achieved an exalted state of sanctity. It means, rather, to have a keen sense of one's own shortcomings and a broad tolerance for those of others. Love II is not a human achievement and is not experienced as such. What is usually experienced instead is the marvel of God's love that sustains and guides us so abundantly far beyond our capabilities or our merits. Vulnerability is one way to characterize compassion. Vulnerability is perhaps best described as caring without controlling. In the wilderness the temptations that come to Jesus are Old Testament prophecies of the status and power, i. e., the ability to control, that would come to him if he would accept those definitions of his messianic role. He could turn stones into bread to feed the hungry, cast himself down from the top of the temple and not be hurt, and have dominion and power over all the kingdoms in the world. In short, he could care and control at the same time, empowering his concern with the ability to manipulate physical reality to serve the concerns. What a neat combination—to care and always be able to do something about it! But Jesus rightly sees this as living according to his own will, rather than the will of God. And he rejects it, for "You shall love the Lord your God and him only shall you serve" (Matthew 4:10).

His love as messiah is powerless in the eyes of the world. He gives himself into the hands of sinful humans, making his witness of omnipotent love and leaving those who hear him free to make whatever response they choose—even to crucifying him. He fulfills a very different type of Old Testament prophecy in his vulnerability—"he opened not his mouth." In doing so, he opens to us the very center of love—to love without reserve, without protection, without armoring ourselves against hurt, without even the means to make our love efficacious—in short, without control. That is vulnerability, God's definition of love in Christ.

Vulnerability is not easy. When we care for others, we want to do something about it. If we have chosen to be in a helping profession, part of our motivation may have been, as the psychoanalyst Allen Wheelis suggested, to nurture others in the ways we unconsciously wish we had been supported, and were not. But then, in the depths of caring for others, to find ourselves helpless to do anything to assuage their suffering is pain indeed. We have saved neither them nor ourselves.

Karl Menninger once wrote that the final maturity required by a psychiatrist was to get over the need to cure (*The Vital Balance: The Life Process in Mental Health and Illness* [Magnolia, Mass.: Peter Smith, 1983]). As long as we are trying to cure others, we are really concerned, not about their unique humanness, but about our own need to control. What the other persons ultimately need is not for us to reassure ourselves that we have the resources to solve their problems, but our vulnerability in listening and paying attention to them as they really are, not as we wish they were. I remember counseling over a long period of time with a man whose commitment to his own growth was matched only by his stubbornness against admitting that it could ever happen. His integrity demanded that he refuse to believe that he could be helped or help himself in any significant way. Small changes did take place, of course, but he steadfastly denied them. Finally it dawned on me to confess to him that I loved him and was unable to help him, that I believed his pain was serious enough that I did not know what to do or if anything could be done to help him. He heard my confession of vulnerability with greater relief. To him it had been the first time in his life that anyone had taken him seriously. Never before had anyone been willing to accept him where he was. What happened, of course, is that he began to change. Now that he did not have to keep on convincing others of his hopelessness, he could begin to look at his life and decide whom he really wanted to be.

It is easy to say to our children or our beloved, "I love you just as you are." But there will come a time, and times, when who they really are forces us, if we are honest, to give up our cherished images of them and of ourselves. Children, in winning their autonomy from us, are especially adept at picking the one spot in our psyche that is non-negotiable. "We're not like our parents, son. If you want to that's all right with us. We love you just the same. But . . ." There is always a "but," something we did not even know we expected, or wish we didn't. But there it is—the limit and the challenge to our vulnerability and the depth of our love. (I am not talking against the values of setting limits to aid in the development of internalized ego controls in the growing child.)

With the one we love most of all the case is equally poignant. We have given our lives to each other; heroically solved the problems of establishing and managing a home together; and settled down, perhaps for years, to the joy and the routine of sharing a life. But she does not stay the same. She continues to grow, but now in a way I do not understand, and that threatens me fundamentally. Or that aspect of her that I never did like, but successfully overlooked, looms larger and larger until it fills the horizon of my consciousness like an angry storm cloud, obscuring everything else. Vulnerability is the issue. Will I let love open up that scarred and scared part of me? Will I give that also to

her, not knowing whether she will heal or destroy it
and perhaps me in the process? Will I give that to her
also, simply because I love her?

Compassion is expressed in gentleness. When I
think of the persons I know who model for me the
depths of the spiritual life, I am struck by their
gentleness. Their eyes communicate the residue of
solitary battles with angels, the costs of caring for
others, the deaths of ambition and ego, and the peace
that comes from having very little left to lose in this
life. They are gentle because they have honestly faced
the struggles given to them and have learned the hard
way that personal survival is not the point. Their
caring is gentle because their self-aggrandizement is
no longer at stake. There is nothing in it for them.
Their vulnerability has been stretched to clear-eyed
sensitivity to others and truly selfless love.

Such is compassion expressed in the prayer of
discernment that completes and includes commitment and freedom. The approaches to prayer
appropriate to this dimension include those appropriate to the others. Active reflection, contemplation,
meditative dialogue with the depths, and blissful
absorption; all are aspects of the graces of prayer
available in the dimension of compassion. But prayer
in this dimension also goes beyond them to co-
creatorship, participation in God's loving healing of
ourselves and creation. *Prayer of discernment* can be
an overall term for the locus of healing of purpose
and a particular term for the prayer life of compassion. Its center is deciding to act to realize God's
purpose in the world. It happens by sitting down each
morning to receive the day fresh from God's hand.
Then we go out and act in faith. Sometimes there may
be a clear sense of leading. Most often there is not.
Sometimes we do not even have the sense that the

silence has been refreshing—only that in boredom and impatience we have suffered through the confusion in our psyche for a while. So it is only in faith that we go out and act. And then we come back to listen to God again. The conscious understanding of the discernment we have received may come very much later in retrospect. Or it may not come at all. No matter, we pray and act, listen and decide, in faith.

The heart of the prayer of discernment is intercession. For prayer is ultimately living out the realization that we are meant to be the community of co-creators with God, bringing the creation to the fulfillment of its promise. To act without the prayerful discernment of God's action would be foolish. To pray and then not to act in co-creation would be empty. Intercession is God's desiring through our desiring the specific healing and redemptive work to which we are called. In discernment we listen for the concrete acts of mission that are given to us. In intercession our passion, our desire is linked to God's desire for that healing and redemption. Sometimes we do not understand why we are prompted to pray for a specific person and cause. Sometimes we do not understand why we are *not* called to pray in a specific situation. Often there is no visible effect of our prayer; sometimes there is a dramatic one. It makes no difference—intercession is the way we live our vocation to manifest God's love, living our faith.

The prayer of discernment is an active, intentional focusing of reality in the service of love. Lawrence LeShan, in *The Medium, the Mystic, and the Physicist*, writes about prayer for healing in words that help describe how prayer is an act of compassion:

The healer knows that he is part of the whole cosmos as a
wave is part of the ocean. There is no separation between
him and the rest of the universe, yet he is a unique part,
the All affects him as he affects the All. The healee is also
part of the All. The healer is, so to speak, another wave.
In this state of consciousness, the healer knows that he is
distinct from the healee, although both are part of the
same ocean and thereby connected. In moments of the
pure knowledge of this, the healer mentally tends to
bring the immense resources of the harmonic energies of
the cosmos to bear on the healee and thus to increase his
inner and outer harmony.

As an act of love, prayer is a courageous act. It is a
risk we take. It is a life-and-death risk, believing in
the promises of the gospel, that God's love is indeed
operative in the world. In prayer we have the
courage, perhaps even the presumption and the
arrogance or the audacity to claim that God's love
can be operative in the very specific situations of
human need that we encounter.

It was suggested earlier that prayer can be thought
of as reframing. In the prayer of discernment, we
receive a name or theological insight for God's
purpose for us in this moment or this day or this
lifetime. By grace we are sometimes able to freely
choose this purpose as our own purpose, enlarging
and healing our former understanding. We choose
this larger purpose by deciding to act upon it, and
thus manifesting or displaying God's love by changing our behavior in some modest way in this sensory
reality. The decision is an intimate dialogue between
conscious and unconscious toward that end. Not only
our conscious thinking and doing, but our nervous
system below conscious awareness, and indeed our
whole organism, participate in that enterprise.

Prayer of discernment is, then, a reframing,
because when the purpose or context changes, the

behavior changes. The behavior changes, not because we consciously will and control different actions, but because more graceful and loving behavior flows out of the conscious and unconscious transformation of purpose. Conscious control is much too limited a strategy for living compassion. The prayer of discernment invites God's reframing of purpose which alone can effect the transformation of behavior that we recognize as compassion when we see it.

# CHAPTER TWELVE

# Prayer in Ministry

Prayer is how the healing of purpose takes place in our time. If we can transcend our Newtonian notions of time, we can imagine the possibility that God calls us as immediately and powerfully as Jesus formed that first unlikely community of disciples. If God does call us to mission and ministry, it happens through prayer.

But prayer is not credible to us as nonbelievers of the Enlightenment or as affluent nonpersons in the solidarity of the world community. As Enlightenment nonbelievers we are trapped in a mechanical, materialistic, deterministic world which has no believable place for the God who walked on the beach and healed the purpose of Peter and James and John. Our liberal theology preserves a tepid accommodation in the world of Newton's physics for our subjective religious fantasies, as long as we do not accord any reality to them. But ironically some scientific findings themselves radically call that mechanical world view into question as the final word on the nature of reality. We can find in ideas like the holoverse magnificent new ways of making sense of God's reality in the world. In contemporary understandings of self, mind, and human willing, prayer becomes excitingly real. We can be liberated from our theology and the obsolete world view to which it accommodated and discover anew that God indeed heals our purpose and calls us to mission and ministry through prayer.

Prayer can reunite affluent nonpersons in the solidarity of the world community. In the holoverse we are more fundamentally one than we are separate, isolated selves in sensory reality, denying our kinship with those of other classes, races, nations. In prayer as reframing, we dialogue with our unconscious depths, meeting there our fundamental formation in the community of humanity and spirituality and sexuality which transcends our individual separateness.

Prayer enlivened by these contemporary cultural resources can integrate and fulfill historic earlier metaphors for the healing of purpose. The metaphor of doing ministry, illustrated in Dewey's thought, contains the essential insight that God's healing of purpose comes in naming and deciding. God's call comes in action verbs. Prayer is that process by which we hear the name for our vocation, our purpose, and decide to realize it in action. In doing ministry we are transformed as our purposes are aligned with God's purpose for us. We do ministry by praying as we understand the fullness of that metaphor.

The metaphor of knowing God, illustrated in Calvin's thought, is also an essential aspect of prayer. Calvin insisted that we can only know the true reality of the world and of ourselves as God in Christ, through grace, reveals it to us. Prayer is that essential process through which grace comes. By grace we have the discipline to wait before the Lord. By grace our minds are liberated from the self-deceiving illusions by which we have lived. And by grace we are able finally to know and live God's love.

Prayer is also the expression of Augustine's fundamental insight that the central issue of faith is loving God. God's love for us is the central message of the gospel. Our transformation in and through Christ, so that our loves find their proper place or weight in God, is the end of faith. Prayer is that mysterious and graceful act by which we receive God's love and are enabled to love ourselves. Growth in prayer is growth in love. Prayer is the reception and the expression of love.

Unfortunately, in contemporary Christian usage, prayer is often an isolated, even a trivial activity. It is too often a habitual blessing for an otherwise unrelated activity. Or it is thought to be necessarily expressed in spoken or written words, sent over unimaginable distances to God, who otherwise would not know what we had in mind. If prayer is to be a metaphor for the healing of purpose, it needs to be lived in its depth and richness and complexity. It must be the center of our Christian community and personal experience. The prayer of commitment is an expression of the church as collective authority and treasure store of images and symbols, forming persons by the wisdom of the tradition. It is prayed by persons desiring to be formed in faith and conformed in will to Christ. The prayer of freedom immerses us in the fullness and void of God's mysteries, blowing away our narrow definitions of self and community. It is prayed through us by a Christ greater than we could possibly imagine, taking us beyond the boundaries we have set for ourselves. The prayer of compassion is love; the love of infinite God for us, and the love by which the world community participates in God's redeeming love until all are brought to the fullness promised in Christ. Love finally is the ground, the aim, and the means of prayer.

Prayer is not only something we do, it is who we are. It is how God heals and makes whole our partial and contaminated purposes, so that we may be, as community and as persons, who God intends us to be.